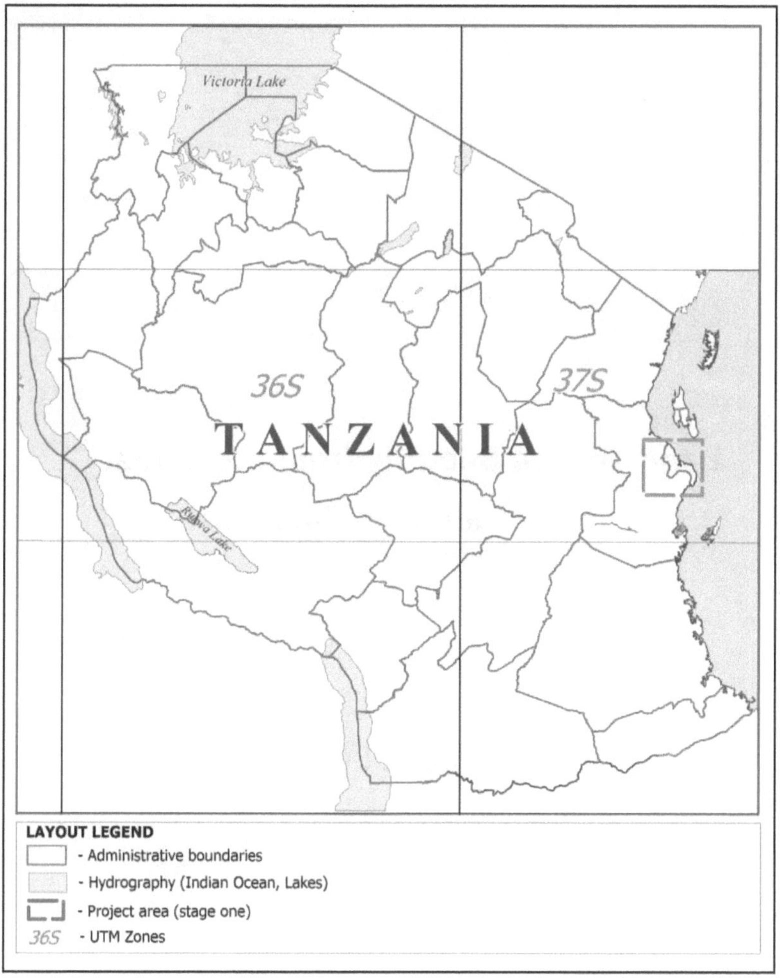

LAND REFORMS OF TANZANIA

Land Tenure Security from pre& post Independence in Tanzania

by

Dr. Furaha Lugoe

Acronyms and Abbreviations:

ARIDA-   Ardhi Institute, Dar Es
Salaam
ARIMO-   Ardhi Institute, Morogoro
ARITA-   Ardhi Institute, Tabora
ASDP-   Agricultural Sector
Development Programme
ASDS-   Agricultural sector
Development Strategy
BOT   Bank of Tanzania
CASLE   Commonwealth Association
of Surveying and Land Economy
CBO -   Community Based
Organisation
CCRO   Certificate of Customary
Rights of Occupancy
CO-   Certificate of Occupancy
CoL   Commissioner of Lands
CSO   Civil Society Organizations
CVL   Certificate of Village Land
DCF -   District Compensation Fund

DDC   District Development Council

DDD   District Development Director

DIP-   Disease, Ignorance and
Poverty

DLB -   District Land Board

DLHT -   District Land and Housing
Tribunal

DLO-   District Land Office

DSM   Director of Surveys and
Mapping

EDF-   European Development Fund

ESRF   Economic and Social
Research Foundation

EU-   European Union

FY   Fiscal Year

GIS   Geographical Information
System

GoT   Government of Tanzania

GPS   Global Positioning System

HDI-   Human Development Index

HHSD   Housing and Human
Settlements Development

HIPC-	Highly Indebted Poor Countries

HRDS-	Human Resources Development Survey

HSD	Human Settlements Division

HSDD	Human Settlements Development Division

HSP	Human Settlements Policy

ICT	Information and Communications Technology

IHL-	Institutions of Higher Learning

ILO	International Labour Organization

IST	Institution of Surveyors of Tanzania

JAS	Joint Assistance Strategy

KRA	Key Result Area

LA	Land Act

LAC-	Land Allocation Committee

LAI-	Land Administration Infrastructure

LAIF	Land Administration Infrastructure Fund
LAS-	Land Administration System
LASS -	Land Administration Support Services
LDS	Land Delivery Services
LDSD-	Land Development Services Division
LGA	Local Government Authority
LGRP	Local Government Reform Program
LIS	Land Information Systems
LSDS-	Lands Sector Development Strategy
LTS-	Land Tenure System
LUMO -	Land-User Ministries and Organizations
MAFS-	Ministry of Agriculture and Food Security
MDA	Ministries, Departments and Agencies

MDG	Millennium Development Goals
MIC	Ministerial Implementation Committee
MIS-	Management Information System
MJCA-	Ministry of Justice and Constitutional Affairs
MKUKUTA	Mkakati wa Kukuza Uchumi na Kupunguza Umaskini Tanzania
MKUZA	Mkakati wa Kuondoa Umaskini Zanzibar
MLHHSD	Ministry of Lands, Housing and Human Settlements Development
MLHSD	Ministry of Lands and Human Settlement Development
MNRT-	Ministry of Natural Resources and Tourism
MoF -	Ministry of Finance
MP	Millennium Project
MP	Member of Parliament

MPEE   Ministry of Planning, Economy and Empowerment

MRALG   Ministry of Regional Administration and Local Government

MTEF-   Medium Term Expenditure Framework

MWLD   Ministry of Water and Livestock Development

NACSAP   National Anti-Corruption Strategy and Action Plan

NAO-   National Accounting Office

NCMIS-   National Centre for Mapping Infrastructure and Services

NCPS-   National Council Of Professional Surveyors

NEMC   National Environmental Management Council

NGO -   Non – Governmental Organisation

NHC   National Housing Corporation

NLAC -   National Land Advisory Council

NLP   National Land Policy of 1995

NLUPC -   National Land Use Planning
Commission

NSDI   National spatial data
Infrastructure

NSGRP   National Strategy for Growth
and Reduction of Poverty

NVRS-   National Village Resettlement
Scheme

ODA   Overseas Development
Assistance

PA-   Professional Association

PAF   Performance Assessment
Framework

PAF   Performance Assessment
Framework

PBFP   Property and Business
Formalization Program

PDRF   Plot Development Revolving
Fund

PEACE   Public Education, Awareness
Creation and Enhancement

PER   Public Expenditure Review

PIC-   Presidential Implementation
Committee

PILL-   Program of Implementation
of the Land Laws

PMO   Prime Minister's Office

PMO-RALG PMO-Regional
Administration and Local Government

PO-PSM   President's Office-Public
Service management

PO-RALG   President Office – Regional
Administration and Local Government

PPA-   Participatory Poverty
Assessment

PPP   Public Private Partnership

PRBS-   Poverty Reduction Budget
Support

PRS   Poverty Reduction Strategy

PRSC   Poverty Reduction Support
Credit

PRSP-   Poverty Reduction Strategy
Paper

PSCP   Private Sector Competitiveness Project

RCSSMRS Regional Centre for Services in Surveying Mapping and Remote Sensing

RDD   Regional Development Director

RDS-   Rural Development Strategy

RLDO-   Regional Land Development Office

RO-   Right of Occupancy

RoT   Registrar of Titles

RRP   Regional Restructuring Program

SMD -   Surveys and Mapping Division

SPILL   Strategic Plan for the Implementation of the Land Laws

SSS   Sites and Services Scheme

SUA-   Sokoine University of Agriculture

SUDP-   Strategic Urban Development Plan

SWG   Sector Working Group

SWOT-   Strengths, Weaknesses, Opportunities and Threats

TACAIDS   Tanzania Commission for AIDS

 TANAPA-   Tanzania National Parks Authority

TATP-   Tanzania Association of Town Planners

TIC   Tanzania Investment Centre

TIVEA-   Tanzania Institute of Valuers and Estate Agents

ToC-   Team of Consultants

ToR-   Terms of Reference

TP-   Town Planning

TP(D)   Town Planning (Drawing)

TRD   Tropical Research and Development

UCLAS   University College for
Lands and Architectural Studies
UDEM   Urban Development
and Environmental Management
UDSM-   University of Dar es
Salaam
UN   United Nations
UNDP   United Nations Development
Program
UNMP   United Nations Millennium
Project
URT   United Republic of Tanzania
VLA   Village Land Act
VLC-   Village Land Council
VLUP-   Village Land Use Plan
VPO-   Vice President's Office
WCR   Warioba Commission Report
WHO   World Health Organization

Chapter 1: INTRODUCTION

In the broadest sense, land involves the whole morphological landmass together with developments thereon. Tanzania is a vast territory of diverse climates and ecosystems hosting the continent's great lakes, plains and mountain ranges and yielding an enviable blend of vegetation and agricultural products. Tanganyika was a self governing land of communities long before the historical Berlin Conference of 1884. The land was vested in communities and land control was the primary objective for the sustenance of each family and communities providing individual and collective needs of the communities. The communities fell under colonialism and became a German colony from 1884 to 1917 and a British Protectorate from 1918 to 1961. Tanganyika gained political independence from the British on 9th December, 1961 and became a Republic in 1962. Zanzibar became independent on 10th December, 1963 and the People's Republic of Zanzibar was established after the Zanzibar Revolution of 12th January, 1964.The two sovereign states joined to form one sovereign country - The United Republic of Tanzania (URT) on 26th April, 1964. Land in the URT is however, not among the list of matters comprising the union as Zanzibar regulates its land differently from Tanzania mainland. Henceforth, therefore, references to Tanzania should be taken to mean Tanzania mainland unless otherwise stated.

Location,

Tanzania is located in Eastern Africa between Longitudes 29^0 and 41^0 East, and Latitudes 1^0 and 12^0 South. The country is bordered by Kenya and Uganda in the North; Rwanda, Burundi and Democratic Republic of Congo in the West; Zambia and Malawi in the South West; Mozambique in the South and the Indian Ocean in the East. Zanzibar is located in the Indian Ocean approximately 30 kilometres from Tanzania Mainland, North East of Dar es Salaam.

Land Size

The URT is the 31st largest country in the world, 13th largest country in Africa and the largest country in the East African Community (EAC). The country covers a total dry land area of 886,100 square kilometres of which Tanzania Mainland covers 883,600 square kilometres and Zanzibar covers 2,500 square kilometres. With the exception of a few mountains, most of the country forms a plateau lying between 120 metres to 1,650 metres above sea level. Water bodies cover a total of 61.5 square kilometres and comprise the following major lakes: Victoria (34.9 sq.km.); Tanganyika (13.4 sq.km.); Nyasa (5.6 sq.km.); Rukwa (2.8 sq.km.); and lake Eyasi (1.0 sq.km.). Other water bodies, on land mass (small lakes, dams, rivers, etc.), cover 3.8 square kilometres. Major Islands in Tanzania Mainland are: Mafia island (518 sq.km.) and Ukerewe (64 sq.km). The country has more than 32 mountains including the world famous Mount Kilimanjaro, the tallest mountain in Africa standing at 5,895 metres above sea level. Tanzania has a total of 16 National parks and game reserves covering a total area of 57,365 square kilometres. The largest national parks are the Ruaha national park (20,300sq.km) and the Serengeti National park (14,763km^2.)

Demography

According to the 2012 Population and Housing Census, the population of Tanzania (including Zanzibar) is 44,928,923 people. Tanzania mainland has an estimated population of 43.6 million people of which 21.2 million people are males and 22.4 million people are females. The population is diverse and composed of about 120 tribes. The average household size is 4.8 persons while the sex ratio is 95. The population of Tanzania has grown rapidly from 12.3 million in 1967 to 17.5 million in 1978, 23.1 million in 1988, 34.4 million in 2002 and 44.9 in 2012. The population of Tanzania has more than tripled from 12.3 million people in 1967 to 44.9 million people in 2012. The largest city, Dar es Salaam accounts for 10 percent of the total Tanzania Mainland population and is now rated as the tenth fastest growing city in the world. In ten years (2002 to 2012), the population of Tanzania increased by 30 percent from 34.4 million to 44.9 million. Although the country remains sparsely populated, the population density of the country has grown dramatically from 25 persons per square kilometre in 1988 to 38 persons per square kilometre in 2002 and 49 persons per square kilometre in 2012. It is estimated at the current annual population growth rate of 2.7 percent, the population of the country will double in the next 26 years. The age distribution of the population is skewed to the young population and children who form 44.2 percent of the population.

Land Use

About 70% of Tanzania can be classified to lie in arid and semi arid regions geographically; and (iii) both the NLP and ALP acknowledge that about 75% of the land area in Tanzania is difficult to manage because of either difficult relief, tsetse flies, unreliable rainfall, national parks, game and forest reserves and mountains.

Arable Land

Statistics provided by both the national land policy (NLP) of 1995 and the agriculture and livestock policy (ALP) of 1997 show that slightly less than 50% of Tanzania's land mass is comprised of arable land. A total of 44 million hectares of land are suitable for agricultural production, but only 10.8 million hectares are cultivated mostly under subsistence agriculture. The latter consists of smallholder farmers cultivating between 0.2 and 3.0 hectares. The potential exists for expansion of agricultural area under cultivation for small, medium and large-scale farming in areas with available land for expansion. The picture being painted by this statistic is that there is ***abundant arable land for agriculture for the foreseeable future***. But, of all sectors in the economy, agriculture land use has been stagnant for many years. Poverty and human development report 2009 shows that the sector has shown growth rates of 4.4% since 2000, well below MKUKUTA's target of 10% by 2010 and the sector's contribution to the economy declined to 24% in 2008. The report also states that "a significant proportion of households have consumption levels not far from the poverty line. Households too are diversifying out of agriculture to improve well-being." Among all the world's countries, Tanzania's gross domestic product (GDP) is the fifth most dependent on agriculture—about 45%. At least 76% of the population works in the agricultural sector. Tanzania has the world's 18th lowest rate of urbanization: just 25% of its people live in urban areas. Against this backdrop, most Tanzanian farmers work very small plots and grow food mostly for domestic consumption. Low productivity on these farms is endemic. According to the World Food Program, more than 40% of Tanzania's population lives in chronic food-deficit regions. The extreme prevalence of HIV/AIDS, which infects 6.2% of the country's adult population, compounds the effects of poor productivity and hunger. At least 38% of children under five in Tanzania are chronically malnourished (that is, their height is stunted for their age), and more than 50% of children suffer stunted growth in over 30% of all regions in the country.

Pastureland and Rangelands

Out of the total 88.52 million hectares of national land resource, 60 mill hectares are rangelands ideal for livestock grazing with carrying capacity potential of 20 million livestock Units. However, due to tsetse infestation which is estimated to occupy 40% of the total land, its full potential has not been fully realized. Out of the 60 million hectares, only 35.5 mill ha, (or 57.9%) is permanent. Further, the land area used for pasture stands at about 44 mill ha, which is greater than the permanent pasture land available. These figures imply that a sizable proportion of grazing is undertaken on non-permanent 8,47 mill hectares of pasture that, as experience has shown, is vulnerable to harsh weather and climatic conditions. It is argued that sustainable livestock keeping can only be possible where land use suitability is considered. In this case, it is possible on permanent pasture implying that a sizable herd will have to graze in ecosystems located outside the permanent pasture.

Forests and Wildlife

Forests and woodlands cover about 45 million hectares of Tanzania's land surface [1], half of this resource is on unreserved public land. Most of the forest is savannah and intermediate woodland. The wildlife of Tanzania is a unique natural heritage and resource that is of great importance both nationally and globally. Some 19% of her surface area devoted to wildlife in protected areas where no human settlement is allowed and 9% wildlife co-exists with humans to a total of 28%.

---

[1] In Africa, more than 70 percent of the population depends on forests and woodlands for its livelihood; one fifth of rural families' daily needs come from forests. Woodlands and forests supply approximately 60 percent of all energy. Forest-related activities accounts for a large part of the GDP of most of the continent's countries.

Background of Land Tenure Systems

Before the advent of colonialism in Tanganyika, land was held by the indigenous people in tribal or ethnic groupings under tribal chiefs, clan heads and village elders. Land was communally owned and chiefs, headmen and elders retained powers of administering the lands in trust for their communities. The individual as a member of a family, clan or tribe acquired rights to use the arable land he and his family could clear, cultivate and manage. When the land showed signs of exhaustion, then shifting cultivation was practised. In many of these areas, there was and there is still communal land for grazing and forest lands for cutting firewood. This type of land cultivation and shifting agriculture was acceptable under conditions prevailing by then of low population densities, land abundance and subsistence level agriculture.

Tanzania was under German colonial rule form 1884 to 1916 and British rule from 1917 to 1961. The country attained its Independence in 1961. By virtue of the Imperial Decree of 1895 all land in *Deustch-Ostafrika* (i.e. German East Africa which included Tanganyika, Rwanda and Burundi), whether occupied or unoccupied was declared 'un-owned crown land' vested in the German empire, save for claims of ownership by private persons, chiefs or native communities which could be proved. The decree, therefore, vested radical title to land in the German empire. A distinction was made between claims and rights to occupy land. Claims were to be proved by documentary evidence while occupation by cultivation and actual possession of the land. In practice only settlers engaged in plantation agriculture such as sisal, coffee, rubber and cotton could prove title to land and enjoyed security of tenure. The indigenous people could not prove ownership. Hence, they were left with permissive rights to occupy the land. Under the German colonial administration, the land of Tanganyika was mainly used to foster settler interests. Freehold Titles were issued to promote large scale land alienation for plantation agriculture run by settlers. By the end of First World War some of the best lands in the highlands and farms amounting to 1,300,000 acres had been alienated in favour of foreigners. Under British Colonialism, the system of land holding changed, albeit slightly. Following the enactment of the Land Tenure Ordinance No. 3 of 1923 (Cap 113), all land in Tanzania 'whether occupied or unoccupied' was declared 'public land'. This Ordinance introduced the concept of 'Rights of Occupancy' in the country which, in essence was a duality in the land holding comprising the granted 'Right of Occupancy' which was issued with a paper title and the 'Deemed Right of Occupancy' under which customary land was held and no paper titles were issued; hence the latter type of land holding was automatically entrenched with lesser security of tenure. Under this new land tenure system, radical title to land was vested in the Governor of Tanganyika to be held, used or disposed of as Rights of Occupancy for the benefit of the indigenous people of Tanzania. In an attempt to protect native rights in land, in 1928, a Right of Occupancy was redefined to include the 'title of a native community lawfully using or occupying land in accordance with customary law'.

The word native was defined to mean any 'native of Africa not being of European or Asiatic origin or descent and includes a Swahili but not a Somali'. The Ordinance, however, failed to protect native rights in their land because it could not prevent large scale and indiscriminate compulsory acquisition of native lands by the colonial government for the benefit of immigrants. After independence, the land administration continued to be carried out under the colonial Land Ordinance, Cap 113 of 1923. The only amendment that was done was to vest radical title to land in the President of the United Republic of Tanganyika instead of the Governor. The Government retained the Right of Occupancy type of land tenure which has the following 'incidents of the Right of Occupancy': there is a definite term for the occupation and use of the land; the land must be developed in accordance with preset development conditions; the holder of the land has no right to subdivide, transfer or mortgage the land without the prior consent of the Commissioner for Lands; the holder of the Right of Occupancy must pay periodic land rent to the Government and lastly, the President may revoke the Right of Occupancy of the landholder for ' any public purpose' or 'good cause'. In order to avoid the creation of a small landed class after the attainment of independence in 1961, Freehold Titles were converted into leaseholds for a term of 99 years under the Freehold Titles (Conversion) and Government Leases Act (Cap 523) of 1963. This legislation changed freehold titles into government leases, in effect reducing the largest quantum of estate in land, the perpetual and unfettered freehold title to a Government Lease which is a lesser and finite interest in land exercisable for a maximum period of 99 years only. Subsequently, by virtue of the Government Leaseholds (Conversion of Right of Occupancy) Act No. 44 of 1969, all Government leases were converted into Rights of Occupancy. It is noteworthy that Freehold titles that were issued to foreigners by the German and British governments and subsequently converted to Government Leases and Rights of Occupancy in 1963 and 1969 are still active and have a residual life of around 46 years to-date (2015). Following the promulgation of the Arusha Declaration in 1967, the country fervently sought pursues of its brand of socialism encapsulated in the 'Socialism and Self Reliance' or 'Ujamaa' doctrine. The Villages and Ujamaa Villages Act No. 21 was passed by parliament in 1975 giving powers to Village Governments to acquire and plan land within their boundaries. The villagisation programme created nucleated settlements in many parts of the country. In the implementation of this programme, people were removed, sometimes forcibly, from their isolated hamlets and homesteads and were brought to live together in designated nucleated settlements, mostly along roads. By 1979 there were about 15 million people living in 8,300 Registered Ujamaa and Development Villages on mainland Tanzania with a population of 250-500 families or 1,500 - 7,500 people per village, displaced from their ancestral lands.

In 1990's following disquiet on how land was being managed and used in Tanzania, the Government commissioned the preparation of the first National Land Policy, 1995 to guide land administration in the country. Two key pieces of legislation forming a new land administration centrepiece in the country were enacted. Both, the Land Act, Cap 113 and the Village Land Act, Cap 114 were passed in 1999 to govern the administration of urban and rural lands respectively. The effective date for both pieces of legislation was 2001. The enactment of these two pieces of legislation ushered in a number of land reforms which including decentralisation of the administration of village lands to village level; recognition and promotion of land and mortgage markets; introduction of a new land adjudication system and dispute resolution machinery; provision of increased security of tenure through land surveying and titling of urban lands and the introduction of the Customary Certificate of Right of Occupancy (CCRO) in village lands, which essentially was the first quasi-freehold interest in land to be introduced in independent Tanzania. Under the Land Act, Cap 113 and the Village Land Act, Cap 114, land in Tanzania has been formally classified and falls into three broad categories of land. These are: General Land, village Land and Reserve Land. In 2005 the government formulated a strategy to guide implementation of the two Acts of parliament and has since enabled good funding for the cause.

CONSTITUTIONALITY OF LAND AND PROPERTY RIGHTS

Due to the importance of land, land has been classified as a constitutional matter in the United Republic of Tanzania. Article 24 of the Constitution of The United Republic of Tanzania of 1997 states:

(1) Subject to the provision of the relevant laws of the land, every person is entitled to own property, and has a right to the protection of his property held in accordance with the law.

(2) Subject to the provision of sub-article (1) it shall be unlawful for any person to be deprived of property for the purposes on nationalization or any other purposes without the authority of law which makes provision for fair and adequate compensation.

Article 27 (1) goes on to state that "Every person has the duty to protect the natural resources of the United Republic, the property of the state authority, all property collectively owned by the people, and also to respect another person's property." To govern land administration in Tanzania, the Government of Tanzania developed the national land policy in 1995 and then enacted the Land Act, Cap 113 and Village Land Act, Cap 114 in 1999. Implementation of the national land policy and laws is guided by the strategic plan for the implementation of the land laws (SPILL) of 2005..

OTHER OVERARCHING POLICIES

The national land policy of 1995 and subsequent reviews is developed in the context of the need to adhere to national development plans and initiatives, of short, medium and long term character. The following overarching policies have been considered: the Tanzania Development Vision (TDV) 2025, the National Perspective or Long term Plan 2025, the National Strategy for Growth and Reduction of Poverty (NSGRP/MKUKUTA), the Millennium Development Goals (MDGs - 2015), 'Kilimo Kwanza' Resolution (2009), Ministerial Medium Term Strategic Plans, and the National Medium Term Development Plans. Through the Tanzania Development Vision 2025, this agrarian country intends to transform its economy by achieving minimum annual GDP growth of 8% to attain an industrial base that is comparable to that of middle-income countries by the year 2025. Key tenets of the Tanzania Development Vision 2025 include attainment of high quality livelihoods; peace stability and unity; good governance; a well educated and learning society and a strong and competitive economy. The Vision identified key impediments to the country's past visions as including donor-dependence syndrome and a dependent and defeatist development mindset; a weak economy and low capacity for economic management; failures in governance and organisation for development; and ineffective implementation syndrome. Land has been, is and will continue to be, the human habitat on planet Earth. It is a resource that cannot be expanded as human population, the users, do and should therefore be managed with utmost care and as a communal resource. A starting point in national land management policy is focusing on equitable land distribution, and the regulation of such distribution and use. Regulation starts with a framework that consists of agreeable customs, policies, laws and other forms of statutes that establish and provide for land administration, financing, revenue collection, etc by established government structures. Land Regulation is as old as human communities. In Africa, and Tanzania in particular, communities are diverse in their relationships with the land. These relationships have been subjected to involuntary interference for over a century brewing, in the process, many untold land use conflicts. Conflicts emanate therefore, from circumstances that are deep rooted in history when evaluated against current day vision of economic growth, good governance and freedom from poverty.

Figure: Agro-Ecological Zones of Tanzania

Tanzania has five (in 2000) major urban centres, namely; Dar Es Salaam, Mwanza, Arusha, Mbeya, Dodoma and Tanga cities, 16 Municipalities as Regional headquarters and 120 District headquarter towns. In all, the urban areas occupy 1% of the total geographical area even as they are now occupied by close to 15% of population. As urban centres started to attract large populations, propelled by rural to urban

40

migrations, at independence, land started to play an even more crucial role in politics and the management of towns and cities. An enabling regulatory framework in urban centres is desirable as it could unlock the potential for growth in urban economies. On the contrary, weak frameworks are not desirable as could continue to create slums and communities would suffer from its ills. It is the view of the author that there is much to be learnt from the dynamics of land administration policy in Tanzania in order to avoid undesirable experiences. Careful analysis should always be given to the implication of the various policies that touch on land matters. Tanzania has adversely been affected by colonialism, untried socialist politics, experimental policies on rural development, "false decentralization", focus on massive programs in spite of weak capacity and dismal budgets and unchecked rural-urban migrations.

CHAPTER 2: THE VILLAGIZATION ERA

The first Five Year Development Plan sought to achieve rural transformation through village settlement schemes under the so-called Transformation Approach recommended by the World Bank Mission in 1960, whose goal was "to introduce technical, social and legal systems which allow the exercise of modern agricultural techniques based on relatively high productivity and which consequently justify considerable investment in capital." The focus of this approach was towards regrouping or resettling of peasants in new lands through capital-intensive new settlements, which were supervised by government officials. Village settlements were governed by the Villages and Ujamaa Villages (Registration, Designation and Administration) Act

No.21 of 1975. The Act, did not contain any provisions on land tenure and the question of possessory rights to land was not a part of the program. Under the Act the village council of the ujamaa village government was obliged to "take such measures as may be necessary to acquire rights of occupancy in respect of land within the limits of the village and no other person should have any right, title or interest in or over any land within such limits" . Under Directives published in the Government Gazette as G.N. No. 168 it was intended that anyone living in a village would not receive title to land. In other words, customary tenure would cease to exist. The Regulation of Land Tenure (Established Villages) Act, No. 22 of 1992 was instrumental in the relocation of peasants during Operation Vijiji without compensation and hence a cause of land tenure confusion and numerous disputes in Tanzania. This continued until the clauses were held to be unconstitutional and struck out of the statute book by the Court of Appeal of Tanzania at the instance of two peasants in Attorney-General Vs. Akonaay and Lohay . The effects of villagisation on land tenure were the following:

☐ Relocation of scattered households into more compact residential Villages, with a purpose of providing common social services. Such movements alienated people from ancestral lands.

☐ In some places villagisation caused land degradation and environmental damage . Peasant agriculture and agricultural production deteriorated, largely due to tenure insecurity and also due to farmland being far away from the homesteads.

□   Substantive changes in the distribution of land out-of-owner consent occurred among groups and individuals. Many individuals lost their homes and lands in the process without receiving compensation.

□   Replacement of customary land allocation authorities by elected village councils, without a consented instrument for such a change.

The NLP of 1995 was formulated to address land tenure issues brought about by changing conditions of land use over time and safeguard the security of tenure. Top on the list of these changing conditions are: (i) A higher demand for grazing land; (ii) An expanded urbanization that places higher demand on land for settlements, industries and commerce including the expanding land markets; (iii) The need for higher investment in land development and modernization of agriculture and; (iv) environmental conservation. Consequently, some of the overall aims of the NLP are: (i) To streamline land delivery and enhance the security of Tanzania's Land Tenure System; (ii) To encourage optimal use of land and its resources; and (iii) To facilitate a broad-based socio-economic development without overburdening, and hence threaten, the national ecological balance. In the preface to the National Land Policy document, drawn up by the then Minister responsible for Lands, is stated that land problems extend much further than individual claims to tenure rights. They involve other issues such as the economic use of land, rural and urban development, housing, squatting, the quality and security of title, advancement of agriculture and the protection of the environment. The new NLP therefore reiterates and retains the four central land tenure tenets in a modified form that land is publicly owned and vested in the president as a trustee on behalf of the citizens; speculation in land will be controlled; rights of occupancy whether statutory or customary are and will continue to be the only recognized types of land tenure; and rights and title to land under any consolidated or new land laws will continue to be based mainly on use and occupation". Under this system therefore, the land is "not owned" but is vested in the Presidency and availed to users through a leasehold mechanism that is centred in the Minister responsible for Lands, Commissioner of Lands and the land administration system revolving around that office. In this system, the land user briefly owns the land rights and developments made to the land. Land rights can either be granted or deemed to have been granted and certificates are issued and registered to prove the identity of the rights owner. The effectiveness of the NLP and legislation emanating out of this policy hinges on the effectiveness of the land administration system in the country. The NLP and the new land laws (Land Act No.4 and Village Land Act No. 5 both of 1999) have a set of 15 fundamental principles that " … all persons exercising powers are to have regard to … (GoT, 1995)."

VILLAGE LAND ACCESS

The Village Land Act No.5 of 1999 now governs land tenure and access in villages. It divides village land into communal, vacant and customary land. Only Customary land can be issued with a certificate of customary rights of occupancy (CCRO) in the name of the landholder. Land allocated by a village council "whether made under and in pursuance of a law or contrary to or in disregard of any law" is confirmed to be held for a customary right of occupancy. These provisions have promoted the holder of customary right of occupancy from a bare licensee to a rights holder. Under section 20-(1) of the Land Act the law provides that a non-citizen of Tanzania shall not be allocated or granted land unless it is for investment purposes under the Tanzania Investment Act, 1997. It is intended that land for investment purposes will be identified, gazetted and allocated to the Tanzania Investment Centre (TIC) by way of right of occupancy. The TIC will, in turn, grant derivative rights to investors. The Act does not restrict other forms of acquisition of land rights by non-citizens. There is no restriction on purchases from government through auctions or tenders or from the Presidential Parastatal Sector Reform Commission (PSRC) in the process of privatization of public enterprises. Further, a non-citizen may obtain a derivative right from a village council (section 32 of the Village Land Act). Nor is there any restriction placed on purchases, by non-citizens, of rights of occupancy or even customary rights of occupancy in the market place. Further, there is no restriction on purchase by non-citizens of shares in companies holding rights of occupancy. The thrust of the legislation is to enable foreign investors to access land since they are considered agents for development.

URBAN LAND ACCESS:

Land access in urban centres is operational through the plot allocation and titling system. Plot numbers given in the annual reports of the Survey Division for the 1959/60 –1970/71 years were recently assembled and charted as seen hereunder. The chart indicates the supply or outputs in planned and surveyed urban plots. The graph is seen to be rising with time from 720 plots in 1959 to 3,493 plots in 1963 and higher in subsequent years.

Trend in Output of Urban Plots in the 1960s

Assessment of the annual divisional reports shows that the country witnessed an exponential growth in plot production, from 12,000 plots in 1969 to 15,000 in 1972 when it reached a three-decade maximum (MLHSD, 1959-1967). The figure of 15,000 urban plots output, attained in 1970/71, remained the highest output in nearly thirty years in spite of technological backwardness, inferior skills and lower capacity levels of that era.

Supply of Urban Plots under "Madaraka Mikoani" Policy:

The production of urban plots grew in late 1960s and early 1970s alongside demarcations of plots in Ujamaa villages. However, the number of urban plots produced during the time decreased sharply, perhaps pointing to shifted emphasis in favor of more demarcations in Ujamaa villages and at the expense of urban plots. The production of urban plots nearly came to a halt starting 1972/73, with a national average annual output of 2,000 plots only for the over 100 towns of Tanzania. The stoppage is believed to have given impetus to the growth of squatters in Tanzania's urban centres. Today, between 40% and 70% of Tanzania's urban population in the main urban centres live in unplanned settlements. In Dar es Salaam City it is estimated that the figure is as high as

53

70% of its population. The gloomy scenario with urban plot production in the late 1970s continued into the 1980s as is provided in the chart below. The chart reflects an average annual production of 4480 plots equivalent with the 1965/66 output – about two decades earlier. The plot production numbers decreased at a time when more Government surveyors were available than ever before to undertake the works.

Implications of the "Madaraka Mikoani" Policy

In 1972 Government administration machinery was "decentralized" to the Regions as a result of the Madaraka Mikoani Policy. All land delivery activities were brought under the District and Regional Development Directors, DDD/RDD except the issuance of Title Deeds. It is recalled that Local

Government Authorities were abolished under this policy removing checks and balances on the "decentralization" process. The Ministry of Lands left all plot surveys in the hands of regional staff who were also dealing with urban and village plots with more emphasis on the latter. There was no budget item for surveys at the sector Ministry. As demarcation of village lots went up, that of urban plots went down and before long many towns could not satisfy even 10% of the demand as the Figure below shows. Diminished total output nationally, continued well throughout the 1980s and 1990s until the commencement of the 20,000 Plots project in 2002, three decades later. With the problem growing worse in townships and Dar Es Salaam City in particular, Government sought World Bank assistance and embarked on the Sites and Services Schemes (SSS) as a remedy. But even these remedial programs could not turn the tide under a policy that seriously affected budgeting. As history would have it the Ministry of Lands, and SMD in particular, would be forced to suspend most of its activities and its products would not be made available for physical planning and land delivery in towns for many years to come for lack of a development budget (GoT, 2001). Suspending other activities meant adding insult to injury as production of urban plots had already stalled.

Government Remedial Supply of Urban Land

The Government of Tanzania started financing land development projects just after attaining independence in 1961. Access to decent housing was a political priority issue of the newly independent nation. Hence, the focus was on provision of residential plots in urban areas.

Government started off by providing plots urgently and timely in order to avoid delays in urban development (1961 – 1972).

The problem of urbanization overwhelmed Government efforts at coping with the housing situation as early as mid-1970s and squatters started growing in most urban areas. Government's response was as follows:

☐ Initiating the squatter clearance programs and later squatter upgrading as a means of introducing services.

☐ Sites and services scheme (SSS) was launched under financial assistance of the World Bank, and the National Housing Corporation (NHC) was established. These were seen as moves aimed at addressing land and housing availability for those living in squatters.

☐ The housing finance approach was also attempted by establishing the

Tanzania Housing Bank (THB) to provide cheap loans to the low-income earners. THB died as a result of mismanagement and misguided policies in 1995.

Urbanization continued unabated as life in the villages became harder with people seeking employment in the towns but with the supply of urban plots and housing remaining far below demand. Further Government Efforts included:

☐   The Growth Centre Policy was launched during the Second Five Year Development Plan that included nine major urban centres. The aim was to reduce the pressure on Dar Es Salaam by setting up Growth Centres.

☐   In 1978 the government initiated the planning and survey of more residential plots in Tabata, Mbagala, Kinyerezi and Mbezi areas of Dar Es Salaam City. There were no thorough studies on the demand for plots for particular land use in a given location. For example industrial sites at Kitunda, also in Dar Es Salaam, were never developed as was intended. There were no targeted efforts at supplying urban plots in the 1980s besides those provided to public corporations. The urban centres sprawled by large proportions into village lands and more squatters evolved. In more recent years, Government has attempted to address itself to urban land delivery and land use problems through the 20,000 Plots Project in order to confront problem of scarcity of urban lands in Tanzania's cities. The project also addressed itself to implementing the sector poverty reduction and the anticorruption strategies. Within a year this new project had created 21,800 plots, in addition to other sources, to a total of 25,865 plots, created at a cost recovery policy. This momentum quickly died down such that the 20,000 plots project's output is now not commensurate with the demand. The annual average output of the 20,000 Plots project in its lifetime is approximately 6,000 plots per year, which is but a 1967 record and far below national demand.

Land for Investors - Land Banking

The context of a land bank is covered in the Tanzania Investment Centre (TIC) Act No.26 of 1997 that includes the whole concept of derivative rights and granting such rights to investors. This is a crucial time in land delivery to address policies of poverty reduction and economic growth, mindful of the fact that: (i) despite achievements in national land policy and legal reforms of 1995 to date, there still remain serious difficulties in accessing land in all categories of investment; (ii) procedures of obtaining land in the villages are cumbersome; and the demand is very high. The demand for land for investment can be assessed from the total number of applications for land lodged with the Tanzania Investment Centre. On the average TIC registers 270 applications annually on a backlog of over 4,200. The list of applications for land parcels at TIC, as judged by the number of acreages, suggests that land is needed mostly for agriculture, livestock development, hotel construction, tourism, manufacturing, processing plants, commercial buildings and apartments. The amount of foreign direct investment (FDI) in the applications ranks as follows: Manufacturing 21 %, Commercial buildings 10 % Agriculture and livestock; construction; tourism; and transport about 9 % of total investment capital each.

THE ROLE OF GOVERNMENT IN LAND ADMINISTRATION:

Government has the leading role in land administration and non-Governmental and professional institutions are its close partners. The reasons for the government's key role include: Firstly, that land and property rights are of central importance in governance and good governance dictates that an important resource such as land must be administered as a collective asset and be managed under the premise that as population grows the territorial jurisdiction remains the same, as land cannot be created. Secondly, land administration is a public good as lives and the economy depend on it and as a collective asset that it is, land administration is a public expenditure that must be budgeted for by the national treasury, and where necessary, to be supplemented by user fees and donations, with government being the collecting and disbursement channel. A key aspect of the land tenure system of Tanzania as provided in the Land Act no. 4 and the Village Land Act no. 5 of 1999 is the enhancement of the rights of vulnerable groups (women, children, minorities) in society. Both Land Act No. 4 and Village Land Act No. 5 of 1999 have attempted to put into effect the above statements with provisions relating to repugnancy of customary law, acquisition of land rights and sales or assignments of land and mortgages. The Village Land Act provides for a representation of women (at least 25%) on the Village Council, at least 4 members of the Village Adjudication Committee and at least 3 on the Village Land Council (dispute settlement) to guard against discrimination in the access to land. Both Land Acts contain gender-neutral provisions on acquisition of land rights in Tanzania. Thus it is open to any man or woman, being a citizen of Tanzania, to apply for granted right of occupancy or customary right of occupancy. Another innovation in this regard relates to the concept of co-occupancy between spouses. Section 161 of the Land Act contains a presumption that spouses will hold the land as occupiers in common in all cases where a spouse obtains land under a right of occupancy for the occupation of all spouses. In every such case the Registrar of Titles is required to register the spouses as occupiers in common. So in an appropriate case an application for a granted right of occupancy by a spouse may lead to registration of both spouses and all spouses as occupiers in common. In addition a spouse's contribution of labor to the productivity, upkeep and improvement of land held in the name of one spouse only leads to acquisition of interest in that land by the other spouse.

FUNDAMENTAL PRINCIPLES

There are fifteen Fundamental Principles of the National Land Policy, which appear as sections 3 (1) and 3 (2) of Part II of the Land Act No.4 and Village Land Act No. 5 of 1999. As stated in section 8.6 above, the NLP and new land laws expect that all persons exercising powers are to have regard to the fundamental principles of the policy and laws. This means that land administration in Tanzania will be guided by the following fifteen statements:

> (a) To recognize that all land in Tanzania is public land vested in the President as trustee on behalf of all citizens;

(b)   To ensure that existing rights in and recognised long standing occupation or use of land are clarified and secured by the law;

(c)   To facilitate an equitable distribution of and access to land by all citizen;

(d)   To regulate the amount of land that any one person or corporate body may occupy or use:

(e)   To ensure that land is used productively and that any such use complies with the principles of sustainable development:

(f)   To take into account that an interest in land has value and that value is taken into consideration in any transaction affecting that interest,

(g)   To pay full, fair and prompt compensation to any person whose right of occupancy or recognised long-standing occupation or customary use of land is revoked or otherwise interfered with to their detriment by the State under this Act or is acquired under the Land Acquisition Act; provided that in assessing compensation land acquired in the manner provided for in this Act, the concept of opportunity shall be based on the following: - (i)market value of the real property; (ii)disturbance allowance; (iii)transport allowance; (iv)loss of profits or accommodation; cost of acquiring or getting the subject land; (v) any other cost, loss or a capital expenditure incurred to the development of the subject land: and interest at market rate will be charged.

(h)   To provide for an efficient, effective, economical and transparent system of land administration

(i)   To enable all citizens to participate in decision making on matters connected with their occupation or use of land

(j)   To facilitate the operation of a market in land;

(k)   To regulate the operation a market in land so as to ensure that rural and urban small-holders and pastoralists are not disadvantaged;

(l) To set out rules of land law accessibly and in a manner which can be readily understood by all citizen;

(m) To establish an independent, expeditions and just system for the adjudication of land disputes which will hear and determine cases without undue delay;

(n) To encourage the dissemination of information about land administration and land law as provided for by this Act through programmes of public awareness and adult education, using all forms of media.

(o) The right of every woman to acquire, hold, use, deal with land shall to the same extent and subject to the same restrictions be treated as a right of any adult man.

STRATEGIC PLAN FOR THE IMPLEMENTATION OF THE LAND LAWS, 2005

The logical sequence in the regulatory framework involves policy setting, legislation, strategy and implementation programmes. The land regulatory mechanism in Tanzania reached the strategic planning stage with the adoption of SPILL in 2005. The New Land Laws, provide for a broad classification of land into three categories namely; general, village and reserve lands. Over the period of tenure history in Tanzania, much emphasis has been placed on general and reserve land. Village land has received very little attention in spite of the fact that over 80% of the population lives and operates in villages. Of late, the lack of due attention with regard to tenure security in village lands has tempted many violators to act in contravention of the law. It is therefore appropriate that the plan of action in SPILL has considered mainstreaming village land tenure as a top priority. In order to fulfil its obligations to the users and the economy a land administration system should adhere to three cardinal principles namely; efficiency, effectiveness and economic sustainability. SPILL has been built on the basis of the three principles in the following ways: Efficiency could be attained by: (i) Introducing simple procedures, which can easily computerise. Simplifying procedures is a continuous work, which is dependent on the attitude and preparedness of the staff;

(ii) Providing a broad training to staff to enable especially the staff at district and village levels to attend to a cross-section of issues and duties; (iii) Introducing modern technology. The developed countries are all the time introducing modern technology. Although the officers are well trained 8-10 days per staff member per year are set aside for training purposes; (iv) Co-operate with other authorities. Effectiveness is attainable by decentralising, as much as possible, the functions and activities of the lands sector Ministry. Some duties cannot be decentralized, like the production of the national topographical and framework land-use maps. Large scale maps at 1:1,000-1:5,000 for instance could be dealt with in zones. Municipalities should aim at managing the small scale mapping on their own. But the decentralization must be done step-by-step starting with the most urgent areas.

Economical sustainability of land administration starts with recognition that land has value and land administration should bear its own costs. Initial big investments for buildings, modern equipment and training can probably be provided in partnership with donors. But to run the administration and maintain buildings, equipment and continuously improve the systems have to be financed by fees and taxes or rents from the land. An investment plan has been designed for SPILL. The strategy, SPILL has identified the following nine Key Result Areas, KRAs that are further decomposed, with input from field Consultation meetings, into Strategic principles and Strategic Objectives: (i) Land Tenure, Access and Land Rights;

(ii) Tenure Security, Law and Order, Justice; (iii) Performance of the Land Administration Infrastructure; (iv) Capacity Building; (v) Land Administration Finance, Resource Mobilization and Financial Management; (vi) Land as a Resource, Land Markets, and Public-Private Sector Operations; (vii) Land Management, The Environment and Community-Based Participatory Decision Making and Facilitation; (viii) Performance Monitoring, Regulation, Supervision and Evaluation; and (ix) Public Education, Awareness Creation & Enhancement.

Chapter 3: Land Administration Experience

A 2002 survey of some of the municipalities revealed that there exist a number of problems in the administration of land within the Local Government Machinery. The global figure is that over 70% of land survey offices in the Districts of Tanzania were without professionally qualified surveyors. In Tabora Region for example, it was only Urambo District and the Tabora Municipality that had each a complete team for carrying out land surveys, but the latter had one professional surveyor who was not complemented with technicians and could not therefore function. Tabora, Igunga and Sikonge Districts had no professional surveyors (2001) at all. Nzega District also had one, professional but, did not have technical backup and hence not as productive as would have been. It has been noted that employment was slow and did not match with the demand. In 2001/02 the town-planning department in Tabora Municipality had applied for six posts but only two were granted. The lands sector in LGA seems to suffer from serious budgetary problems. The Municipal authorities seem to leave the town planning departments fetch for own funds. These are only assisted by the retention scheme (RS) and PDRF money from the MLHSD. However, it was noted that difficulties exist for using PDRF money as the recovery plan that relies heavily on approval of TP drawings and on the contributions of developers is quite slow. Late returns attract a penalty. The lands sector suffers from technological problems including an acute shortage of field equipment and vehicles, which the councillors do not seem to understand or even start addressing. The stagnation in the approval of cadastral surveys by SMD was affecting performance in the LGA, which is further complicated by the poor communication between SMD and the survey offices in Districts and municipalities. In the former case for example, Tabora municipality surveyed 1500 plots in 1994/95 only a small portion had been approved by 2001 and others were still pending. A faster response was most desirable. In the latter case, SMD still forwarded approved survey plans to the "Regional Surveyor"- now a non-existent portfolio. These are received by the 'survey advisor to the RAS' and are, in many cases, filed away. It is not easy for the District and municipal offices to know whether or not approval has been granted and hence the plot allocation process is delayed.

Inefficiency in Cadastral Surveys

Coming back to the issue of efficiency of cadastral surveys, it is important to review the entire process of survey instructions and examination of surveys. Several months' delays in approval of cadastral surveys are regressive to the cause. The following need to be revamped: (i) *Survey Instructions*: The three-tire-system of survey instructions in which all three divisions are involved could be reduced to a one step procedure if there can be an agreement on clear regulations on the matter to be administered by one division. After all, the end ought to be the same whoever the administrator of the regulations is and the work is almost entirely of a clerical rather than professional nature. (ii) *Inefficiency in Approval of Surveys*: The issue of speeding up the examination of surveys must be revisited. This is a "catch 22" situation. The SMD was inundated with more surveys for examination than ever before, yet the gross number of new surveyed land parcels and particularly urban plots, was at an all-time low. Prior to the 20,000 Plots project, plot scarcity was explained, partly, by the chaos associated with lack of acquired (fully compensated) land for development. The work done by licensed surveyors had increased as individual persons and businesses continued to seek land for or seek title to land. The examination section at SMD was ever getting busier. (iii) *Enhance Private Sector Participation*: Cadastral Survey output from surveyors was, on the average, decreasing and could so continue to be unless the system focused on process management. There were an average of 85 small jobs received monthly (in 2000) each of which required almost as much examination time. Hence, directives of the chief surveyor to lower level operatives on efficiency had gone without favourable response. It was not uncommon for an examination process to take 6 – 12 months, against the 2 weeks mentioned in directives. As stated earlier, most of the survey jobs were a product of the private licensed surveyors. A viable solution is simply to find a way that will make the licensed surveyors accountable for their products, through a transformation from examination to quality control of surveys, as is being done in most countries. The activity that occupies most of the time of physical planning departments in LGAs is now seen to be the resolution of boundary disputes as people continue to unilaterally uproot and remove boundary beacons contrary to section 11 (1) of the Land Survey Ordinance (CAP 390) and as exemplified under Act No. 18 of 1997. The councillors are rightfully concerned about peace and stability in the neighbourhoods and call upon the authority to replace the beacons as a solution. There are times when the matters go to courts and planners, surveyors, and land officers, playing the expert witness role, are called upon to testify. A mechanism of giving village or ward authorities custody of the boundary and other survey markers should be instituted without delay since survey markers are guarded by law and it is not easy to lay responsibility of their removal on anybody.

Land Registration Records, 2001.
The total number of surveyed land parcels registered with the Records Office of the Surveys and Mapping Division in Dar Es Salaam were not known and

would take time to be determined. A first step hds been accomplished for the city of Dar es Salaam that hosts only 10% of the entire population of Tanzania. Even this knowledge of 78,498 plots and sub urban farms in Tanzania does not shed much light on the owners of the land rights in the City with over 400,000 houses. The office of the Commissioner of Lands reports that some 21,000 plots out of the 78,498 have either offers of titles or both. This is a confusing state of affairs as land administrators do not know how much land was legally delivered and how much is not. Another confusing state is the number of files in the LDSD now (2000) reported to be 197,000 up from 96,000 in 1981. One would assume that there were that many planned and surveyed land parcels in the country. However, revenue projections in the Directorate of Policy and Planning (DPP) use the figure of over 600,000 urban plots, leaving one sceptical as to whether or not such expectations are realistic and realisable. Proper land administration, and particularly, resource allocation, required that the confusion with regard to performance be sorted out as soon as possible. The land allocation process by LGA need be fully reported to the MLHSD to enable the latter monitor the land delivery process at a national level, and take remedial action in policy where one is warranted. A filing system also needs to be sorted out perhaps, using inverse procedures where title records may be used whilst current offers retain provisional numbers until certificates of occupancy are issued. Land administration records ought to be established at zone offices in much the same way as land title records. This calls for a decentralisation of land administration services to the zone headquarters. The numbers of titles registered by the Registrar of Titles in all seven zones as of 20th December 2001 show that there are 118,053 registered certificates of title/occupancy in the country. This number far falls short of approved surveyed land parcels as it seems to indicate that there are only 39,555 such parcels outside the City of Dar Es Salaam. This seems to confirm fears of the LDSD that many people have not wished to register their land rights and could be holding offers to land but not certificates of occupancy. There are also those who hold short-term rights of occupancy that remain valid as long as the owner pays the necessary land rent, yet their numbers and geographical distributions remain unknown. In the interest of a multipurpose cadastre, and increased revenue from land, it is recommended that moves be made to ensure that all registered surveyed land parcels be granted with certificates of occupancy.

Re-Engineering Land Registration
This objective sets out to institute a radical redesign of the land delivery and registration processes in the Land Development Services Division (LDSD) that is headed by the Commissioner of Lands (CoL), so as to achieve a quantum leap in performance and in so doing facilitate the attainment of objectives of the various lands sector laws including the Land Registration Ordinance. Re-engineering aims at improving services at a lower cost both in money and time. It involves more sophisticated procedures, driven by computerisation and employment of ICT tools that produce top-to-bottom organization transformation.

The most significant change in land administration over the last decade, or so, worldwide has been the extent of computerization of the land registries to meet internal requirements for more efficient data storage, more rapid information retrieval, and greater ease in updating the records. Other value-added advantages include: (i) the use of scanning technology to provide **back-up** facilities in case of disaster that can result in loss of data and documents; and (ii) possible *on-line computer access*, via the Internet. The employment of ICT tools is justifiable in terms of (Dale and McLaughlin, 1998): (i) speed (as they significantly outperform current approaches); (ii) suitability (as they are within the financial reach of local professionals and within their range of skills to operate); (iii) appropriate accuracy (matching real needs); and (iv) simplicity of field operations (simple data collection to allow for different field conditions). The land registration and record keeping system of Tanzania is by all standards ripe for re-engineering both at lands sector Ministry headquarters and in the Municipal/Town and District Councils. Problems encountered in the registries and their effects on tenure security and the market are immense. The current system is clogged, inefficient, cumbersome, slow and difficult to store and retrieve documents, hard to debug errors, resistant to information update and cannot be accessed electronically by users. In many ways, the registries do not facilitate the attainment of provisions of the laws on land administration matters. The registry system in Tanzania is both one for land titles and other documents, including mortgages, but works side by side with registry of survey plans in the Survey and Mapping Division and the registry of Town Planning Drawings in the HHSDD. All three are party to land delivery and settlement of disputes. The re-engineering requires the formulation of a joint strategy that includes standards and specifications for technology and other issues in all three Divisions of the MLHHSD. Success of the Village Land Act No. 5 of 1999 is also dependent upon the establishment of Village Registries, which can be established with a focus on an engineered system for efficient and effectiveness to land owners and the market.

Land Dispute Resolutions Mechanisms
Land disputes resolution is cantered around courts and tribunals. People should be given access to tribunals as close to their properties as possible.

Recognising this fact, the Government of Tanzania has enacted the Lands Disputes Courts Act No. 2 of 2002 as an instrument to deal with all such issues. At the lower level, the new system of justice has established land councils and tribunals – village land councils, ward tribunals and District land and housing tribunals. Accessibility to tribunals involves availability of court rooms with appropriate levels of capacity. An efficient system is one in which many disputes are prevented and settled out of courts. More emphasis should be placed on conflict prevention by public awareness creation, and other measures cantered within communities. The NLP has defined a set of fundamental principles as a guideline for the land administration machinery to follow, which if carefully followed should do away with most conflicts and disputes. Conflicts are not conducive to development. They inhibit investment in housing and food production, reinforce social exclusion and poverty, undermine long term planning, and distort prices of land and services. Any land dispute infringes on the security of tenure over land in contradiction to the spirit of the national land policy and new land laws of Tanzania. The strategic advice will take into consideration these well-established facts.

Land Administration and Public Expenditure

The situation analysis in the first, Public Expenditure (PER) study in 2001, made it clear that there is generally, very limited knowledge on the role of the lands sector, particularly by policy makers outside the Ministry of Lands, Housing and Human Settlements Development. To quote one of the conclusions, *"There is limited understanding of the core functions, beyond the seemingly obvious "plot delivery". Indeed the most costly functions of surveys and mapping are least understood. The question thus becomes that of impressing upon Decision Makers that in order to be able to deliver serviced land, survey and mapping is an indispensable undertaking."* The consequences emanating from this fog of diverted focus, as it then appeared to the researchers, were noted, in part, to be a challenge on several fronts namely; (i) Poor land administration and management, (ii) demand for urban plots being greater than supply, (iii) inability to provide serviced land, and (iv) unmanageable urban population growth in relation to physical town planning and in the provision of housing services. Further, in terms of performance it was noted that some key statistics in cadastral surveys, for purposes of delivery of surveyed plots, farms and village lands, show that the situation is **BAD**, and in base mapping the situation is **WORSE**. More so, the freeze in mapping and declining numbers in plots surveyed, even as demand is rising, reveals that the MLHSD is yet to even meet 25% of demand in any area.

Land-Use and Physical Planning

Experiences gained from the recent 20,000 plots project reveal that land delivery is a multi-disciplinary intervention that calls upon several institutions and sub-sectors. Lands sector activities are spearheaded by land-use and physical planning processes that prepare plans for the optimal use of land. The processes unveil soil types, drainage patterns, topographical features, etc, and proceed to zone out the land for specified land-uses. The totality of all of the dry land constituting the territory of the United Republic of Tanzania ought to be included in such a scheme so as to guide investment, markets and settlements whilst conserving the environment for future generations. Land use planning is particularly important to poor economies and the people whose sole asset is the land to which they have access and from which they derive their livelihood. But, land-use planning cannot be undertaken unless the processes are facilitated by data and information that has been well referenced to the ground and to populations through maps and the geo-referencing framework as an essential medium. No wonder PER studies have, all along, underscored the need for investment into geo-referencing and mapping processes for an uninterrupted supply of maps by the sector. SPILL goes a step further as to provide a sequencing chain for the land delivery goal that is built on this framework. It is noteworthy to recall that lands sector professionals have, over the years, called upon the Government to pay particular attention to this aspect of land administration. The 20,000 plots project that started as a project for land delivery in the struggle against corruption in the sector has revealed a very interesting scenario. Out of the investment done so far, about 70% of the resources that remain after compensations have been removed from the total sum has been directed towards providing the geo-referencing framework (survey control), maps (orthophoto imagery) and cadastral surveying. The remaining 30% has been divided up by the activities of physical planning, valuation, advocacy and titling, thus laying emphasis on the multidisciplinary approach and extents of involvement. A similar picture has been revealed in land reform projects undertaken successfully in Thailand, Brazil and Mexico. Experience gained from projects undertaken towards land tenure enhancement in these countries shows that resources committed are basically, divided into four clusters. The clusters are as follows: Petitions and Litigations (6%); Administrative Overheads (12%); Preparation of Records (14%); Mapping and physical planning (28%); Survey Control and Cadastral Surveys (40%). This information is handy in the distribution of resources, cost estimation and budgeting. The need to re-align resources and mainstream activities for the performance of the lands sector has been necessitated by a number of challenges namely; (i) the need to reverse the adverse effects of villagization on land tenure conflicts, sprawling settlements, and agricultural production and pave way to tenure security, and poverty reduction;

(ii) the financial squeeze on the sector activities leading to the freezing of activities in the sector (iii) lack of financing for the village land tenure (implementation of provisions of the Village Land Act No. 5 of 1999); (iv) lack of long term planning in the sector; (v) misguided prioritisation and sequencing patterns in response to inadequate funding. It is noteworthy that Government policy emphasis has now moved from communal services only, to modernisation of agriculture and increased production in context of improved social services for the reduction of poverty. The new mind-set calls for a back-to-the-land policy that facilitates villagers' resettlements to more fertile and larger acreages of land. The new policy framework also calls upon the lands sector to pay more attention to the planning and management of the "small towns" that have now outgrown the village status in population and commercial activity standards. PER studies recommended that prioritisation and sequencing be closely followed in the allocation of budgets. In this regard a table of priorities, similar to the SPILL chart mentioned earlier, had been drawn to guide in the preparation of the medium term expenditure framework, MTEF. With a long backlog of work due to suspension of some activities for over thirty years, wisdom prevailed and the study team recommended a budget scenario *"under which the MLHSD received all that is budgeted for is probably most realistic"*, but also noted that "in the long run the scenario whereby a serious basic needs assessment is done establishes all the requirements of the sector and uses this as basis for budgeting would be better". The latter assumed that the MLHSD addressed all the sector's priority activities, the available resource envelope notwithstanding, with the assumption that past budgeting processes were carried out based on ceilings, thus not reflecting the actual scope of work required to be carried out on the ground.

Chapter 4: PRE-REFORM CHALLENGES

In a statement on his office chalkboard, a reputable Tanzanian economist tells his students and visitors alike that **'exploitation is bad but non-exploitation is worse'**. The exploitation of land resources and generally, the economic use of land and its resources requires the institution of a focused, transparent and rigorous system of land distribution – land administration. Visionary land policies, people-cantered land laws, nationally acceptable strategies and well-equipped land administration machinery facilitate such a system. All developed economies have, with great care and ingenuity, addressed themselves to issues of land reform at one point or another since Napoleonic times and have therefore, successfully built buoyant agriculture and industry upon it. At the centre of the reforms are land rights and security of tenure – two ingredients that Tanzania systematically undermined in the three decades since mid-1960s, and the performance of the land administration system. The inception of reforms and a viable land administration infrastructure requires an across the board recognition of the vitality of the role of land in economic and human development that is contingent on decent earnings by individuals and meaningful state revenue. The starting point is the abundant ultimate resource for human kind – land, the platform of all human activity. Land reform should be directed at: (i) addressing poverty reduction in context of reforms in land administration and resource investment; (ii) tracing historical dynamics with land tenure security in Tanzania; (iii) marginalization of land rights in the villagization programme of the 1960s and 1970s; (iv) subsequent practice and awareness for reform and(v) ushering-in of the national land policy and new land laws. Reforms culminate in a strategic plan and investment plan for the implementation of these laws. The strategy was formulated in a series of validated consultative meetings of stakeholders in 2004/5 and unveils reform messages that every concerned ear must heed to. The messages lead to a proposed ten-year programme of reforms in land administration with known sources of resources. A picture is painted here, of a self-financing sector awaiting the will and resourcefulness of Government to yield results and guide the rural poor out of poverty based on land as the solid platform for human development. Serious and focused land reforms in Tanzania can be tagged to the inception of the National Land Policy **(NLP)** of 1995, whose evolution has a long and rugged history. It is a history that is inundated with underperformance in land policy for over a century. An attempt to formulate a viable land policy required therefore, and of necessity, nationwide debates on the land question and its administration. The **NLP** formulation and the resultant policy document have carefully considered colonial and post-colonial tenure policies set around the Land Ordinance of 1912 and around subsequent 'band aid' amendments to that ordinance including a mixture of freehold, leasehold, customary, feudal and state-controlled provisions instituted after independence. The **NLP** document has also addressed itself to aspects of a modern socio-economic setup and the new world order. Central to the uniqueness of the land policy document is consensual agreement on a set of fifteen fundamental principles that have provided the framework for the new land laws and land administration. Cutting a long history short, it suffices to say that the land tenure practice in Colonial Tanganyika was such that indigenous lands were treated as 'not owned'. The titles in these lands were presumed to have been vested in the State except for lands alienated to settlers under documentary titles. In short, there is very little that has changed in independent Tanzania. In a period of over 40 years of independence, the Tanzania Government has maintained almost the same colonial land policy and practices introduced by the colonial machinery, with some minor reforms and amendments to the Land Ordinance and supporting legislation.

INITIAL LAND REFORMS:

Some major reforms were introduced in 1963 when the Freehold titles were converted to Government leaseholds. The effect of these changes was to reduce interest in land from being perpetual to a definite period with a maximum term of 99 years. In 1965 the Rural Farmlands (Acquisition and Regnant) Act was passed enfranchising the *Nyarubanja* tenants to do away with feudal tenure in Kagera Region. This Act was amended in 1968 to include various types of customary tenants. The amendment was later extended to cover feudal tenancy in Pare, Moshi and Tukuyu districts in 1969. The piece of legislation was meant to address itself to a situation where the landholder was not granted land rights and, whilst in some form of tenancy relationship with the landlord, used and developed the land despite denial of statutory rights. In the same year,

Government leaseholds were converted into rights of occupancy and land rent and development conditions, similar to those pertaining to a normal right of occupancy, were attached to all leases.

REFORMS EMBEDDED IN THE NATIONAL LAND POLICY, 1995:

In spite of corrective measures introduced after independence, by the late 1980s more faults had been identified in post-colonial land policy and practice enough to necessitate an overhaul of the land tenure system **(LTS)**. In response, the Government appointed the Shivji Commission to gather views countrywide on the general direction the country ought to take with regard to land tenure, both in rural and urban areas. Results of this commission led to a set of fifteen Fundamental Principles **(FP)**, among other developments, providing a framework for the national land policy.

The **NLP** was extensively debated by the populace including non-Governmental and Civil Society Organisations and subsequently, passed by Parliament in 1995. The enactment of the Land Act no. 4, the Village Land Act no.5 of 1999, the Land Disputes Courts (Tribunals) Act No.2 of 2002 soon followed the adoption of the **NLP** document.

The Villages and Ujamaa Villages Act No. 21 was passed by parliament in 1975 giving powers, among others, to Village Governments to acquire and plan land within their boundaries. Ujamaa villages were off springs of the villagization programme that created nucleated settlements in many parts of the country. In the implementation of this programme, people were removed, sometimes forcibly, from their isolated homesteads and were brought together in designated settlements, mostly along roads. There, each family was given a plot or a piece of land to construct a house and for communal services such as schools. The programme was carried out rather hurriedly and in many instances in an *ad hoc* manner. By 1979 there were about 15 million people living in 8,300 Registered Ujamaa and Development Villages on mainland Tanzania with a population of 250-500 families or 1,500 - 7,500 people per village, displaced from their lands. In 1982 the Ujamaa and Development Villages Act of 1975 was repealed and village settlements were incorporated into Local (District Authorities) Act No. 7 of 1982. The Villagization Programme was instrumental in altering settlements, land use patterns and the landscape of rural Tanzania to what it is today. The effects of villagization on land tenure were adverse and included the following:

- Relocation of scattered households into more compact residential Villages, with a purpose of providing common social services. Yet, in some places it caused land degradation and environmental damage and, at the same time, forced movements and migrations under Ujamaa alienated people from ancestral lands.

- Peasant agriculture and agricultural production suffered, largely due to **tenure insecurity** and also due to farmland being far away from the homesteads.

- Substantive changes in the distribution of land out-of-owner consent occurred among groups and individuals. Many individuals lost their homes and lands in the process without receiving compensation, a prejudice that has now been consolidated by the new land laws.

- Replacement of customary land allocation authorities by elected village councils, without a consented instrument for such a change causing resistance to the new dispensation that continues to this day.

The absence of a comprehensive post-colonial land policy coupled with the ill-effects of the villagization programme, now irreversible under the new land laws, down-graded the security of tenure and opened the door for the proliferation of land conflicts and disputes at a larger scale.

LAND CONFLICTS AND DISPUTES

Rural land-use conflicts have been on the increase especially between traditional pastoralists and traditional agriculturalists in the past two decades. Likewise forestlands, woodlands and wildlife sanctuaries have been violated. Naturally, peasants are expanding their farms and pastoralists are operating without regard for any land boundaries and destroying the environment. Many a village do not recognise Government established boundaries, and have sparked off serious life threatening cross-village conflicts and disputes. There are persistent land disputes, in urban centres also, as a result of rapid expansion of towns from a total urban population of 686,000 in 1967 to approximately 10 million in 2000. Urban areas are encroaching on fertile farming lands. Urban Councils delineate own boundaries with little regard to basic principles of urban and country planning and wilfully include existing village lands. As a result of this malpractice the existing statutory boundaries of most Municipalities (Regional Headquarters) in Tanzania are very extensive and included some 230 registered villages by 2000. There are also conflicts between squatters and customary land rights owners in unplanned areas of urban centres, which now constitute, on the average, about 70% of town areas. To site an example, of Dar Es Salaam City alone, the number of squatter settlements increased to 55 in the late 1990s rising from 43 in the 1980s and only 16 in the 1970s.

LAND TENURE INSECURITY

The Ministry of Lands and Human Settlement Development (MLHSD) has been established to provide the land administration machinery in Tanzania. It is therefore its prerogative to re-examine the existing land administration system in historical context with a focus on land development and poverty eradication. In so doing the major role is to set up a credible land administration infrastructure (LAI) to meet the challenge. In particular, land sector activities of topographical mapping, land-use planning and management, land parcel definition, land registration, land markets and landed property valuation need a new and proper lease of life. The new land laws have been enacted and are yet to be harmonized with the existing sector laws. These are: the Town and Country Planning Ordinance (Cap 378) of 1956; The Land Registration Ordinance (Cap 334); The Land Survey Ordinance (Cap 390) of 1959; The Professional Surveyors Registration Act of 1977; and corresponding subsidiary legislations. Also harmony must be established with laws for other sectors including water, mines, the environment, roads, natural resources, and conservation sectors, etc. The lands sector is as wide as is land-use. It is cross–cutting in nature and affects the performance of all sectors that operate on the land such as agriculture, water, livestock, mining, game ranging, forestry, the environment; land, sea and air transport; to name but the very basic. The land laws, as it is with land-use are also crosscutting, as all land users must adhere to them if high performance is to be achieved and land conflicts and disputes reduced to the very minimum. Recent public expenditure studies for the lands sector have revealed four clusters of problems that must be addressed so as to free the land for a vibrant national economic growth. These are systemic, exogenous, policy-derived, or financial constraints.

Systemic are problems reflecting policies of the past such as villagisation of the 1970s whose results are expensive and sometimes difficult to reverse, gender imbalance, poor enforcement of law and order, and some urbanization and housing policies of the past. **Exogenous Dynamics are** forces like uncontrolled urbanization, population movement and shift to the east, rural-urban migration, lagging urban infrastructure, corruption and the development of spontaneous settlements are developments taking place outside the capacity of the lands sector, or even the nation. **Policy Derived** problems are central to all as problems of limited capacity for policy analysis and planning, inefficiency and stagnation in land delivery, poor enforcement of planning and building regulations, skilled manpower retrenchments, financial indiscipline, unregulated land markets and non-institutionalisation of dispute settlement machinery, weak enforcement of law and order fall in this category. **Financial Resource Constraints** include the near freeze on topographical mapping and land use planning services, a stagnant cadastral survey system, incomplete village boundary survey, a run-down land administration infrastructure, proliferation of irregular settlements and, poorly facilitated law enforcement institutions are some of the core manifestations.

SYSTEMIC LANDS SECTOR CHALLENGES

Like others to be discussed in this paper, systemic challenges have a known origin and effective climate that support their evolution, existence and growth. These are, by and large, born of mind-sets of land administration leaders to want to continue with past policies and regulations in administering land delivery and land-use processes, in spite of the out datedness and inapplicability of the old arrangement. The land administration personnel cling on to the "old order" often, under certain pretexts such as skewed understanding of the relationship between public and private interests in land or lack of appropriate education on issues. Nowhere is this attitude so prevalent as in the administration of village land that is now primarily governed by the Village Land Act No. 5 of 1999 that also includes the Fundamental Principals of the national land policy, NLP, and corresponding regulations and directives. It is increasingly common to encounter decisions made on the basis of villagization policy and laws that were repealed at the time that the new laws were enacted. The study report of the third public expenditure review process

(PER 4) of 2004 contains a long list of such laws. Most notable are the Villages and Ujamaa Villages (Registration, Designation and Administration) Act No. 21 of 1975 and the Regulation of Land Tenure (Established Villages) Act No. 22 of 1992.

Violation of Fundamental Principles

There are several areas of land tenure that are encumbered and need focused intervention. Firstly, the national land policy requires land administrators to "recognize land rights for long term land occupation, or use" and that these be secured by law. However, participants to various seminars on land administration have witnessed to cases where land rights have not only been ascertained but, land has been taken away from customary and other uses without due compensation in the post-NLP era (Lugoe et al, 2004). Often, the occupier or owner of land does not have a choice and objections are ignored. Secondly, it is well known and acknowledged that land is a scarce resource but, at the same time, one that everyone must, in one way or another, have access to as source of the basic needs of shelter, food and income for all humanity. Land for housing should be facilitated by land acquisition to developers from landowners who are willing to sell or lease out their properties. It is logical to assert that not all people can be landowners and hence mechanisms ought to be put in place aimed at allowing land-use by the landless for the basics of life. Thirdly, provisions should also allow for a third aspect of sustainable land use, namely; short-term leasing of agricultural lands aimed at putting land to productive use in times of economic or other difficulty confronting the landowner. In this regard, a market in land should not only be facilitated but be allowed to flourish also. Land markets should be regulated to guard against speculation and hence protect the poor against loss of this important asset (Lugoe et al 2005). Moreover, mechanisms should be put in place to enable such short-term leases without landowners losing their land rights or being branded as absentee landlords. Finally, the road to women's land rights is still bumpy in spite of pronouncements in the NLP regarding equitable distribution and land access. The male dominant attitudes in traditions and customs, as well as in religious beliefs, are still a part and parcel of the mind-sets in land administration policy to date. There are clauses in the village land act for example, that specifically focus on participation of women in decision making with regard to land administration. A number of critical statements against gender discrimination are provided in the Land Act no. 4, in the context of co-ownership and mortgages (see sections 85, 112, and 161 (2)), which apply to the Village Land Act as well (GoT, 1999a,b). The Village Land Act provides for a representation of women (at least 25%) on the Village Council, at least 4 members of the Village Adjudication Committee and at least 3 on the Village Land Council (dispute settlement) to guard against discrimination in the access to land.

Public Land

Mind-sets of people were grossly confused by the decision to uphold the principle that land vestment in the "sovereign" will continue in independent Tanzania and made "all land in Tanzania to continue as a public good". Confusion reigned when these were followed up with nationalization of assets and property a few years into independence. To many, particularly those who witnessed the events at the time, public land became understood as communal land meaning also that it belongs to everybody (Lugoe et al, 2004). As a consequence of this misconception, land ownership, occupation and land rights for individual citizens took on a secondary and marginal role when viewed in context of group or community rights. The majority of people now still understand, misguidedly, that public land does not give anyone exclusive rights over any land parcel. In practice today, and regardless of the new regulatory mechanisms in place, public land is freely being occupied out of consent. Further, it is arbitrarily occupied and used when: (i) there seems to exist no visible alternative land uses, (ii) the land parcel seems to be vacant, or (iii) authorities do not show up to take administrative or legal action against the illegal occupier. This skewed understanding is a major cause of illegal occupations and use and is hence a cause for untold disputes and conflicts particularly, where a personal need to use land arises. It has been hinted above that land rights include protective rights against alien occupation and trespass, even by authorities that do not carry evidence or granted right to enter land while on government errands. This position ought to be respected by all to minimise untold conflicts and cases of trespass, many of which are ignored by authorities and neglected by law enforcement agencies. Systemic Challenges also include poor enforcement of land regulations and control of planned land developments. Land administration systems are duty bound to create registrable land parcels and appropriately deliver the same in accordance with existing rules and regulations. The onus is on the system to assist the growth of legally accepted land markets and consolidate the security of land tenure. Systemic Challenges manifest themselves in several ways: Firstly, the lacklustre attitude to land administration has led to land scarcity in urban areas and hence has caused people to build in open spaces, hazardous areas and blocking infrastructure. Indifference to procedures causes people to build on or till marginal lands without regulation. Settlements have sprung up as slums, sprawling, unplanned, and poorly serviced and hurriedly constructed, as a result of such marginal performances of lands sector institutions. The slums have attracted the urban poor for providing cheap, though not so healthy, lifestyles. Slums are also conducive to the proliferation of social challenges associated with crime, drugs, prostitution, and other forms of lawlessness. Secondly, there is the issue of unregulated market forces. Properties in irregularly occupied urban lands have marginal values and insecure. They are hard to market because of poor services and accessibility and hence do not contribute much towards sustainable poverty alleviation. Thirdly, is the issue of marginal security of tenure for the majority of properties in slums, as they are erected on land that was neither acquired nor properly granted by urban authorities. Urban authorities view these properties differently. Some are a subject of demolition, with much loss of wealth to owners and the nation. Some properties are upgraded by introducing services and infrastructure. In all cases these remedial actions result in people being disadvantaged through physical displacements from their homes. Often remedial actions such as upgrading irregular tenure therein and servicing the land come late. The cost of upgrading slums is often prohibitively high, much higher than going by the book to acquire, plan, survey, service and deliver land. Upgrading also takes its toll on property losses during demolitions, which are inevitable.

EXOGENOUS CHALLENGES

The lands sector has a particular role to play in the national economy as a distributor of land, guarantor of land rights, solver of disputes and intercessor in land-use conflicts for all land-user sectors, individuals and their businesses.

The sector operates alongside others in ensuring a sustainable socio-economic development, good governance and poverty reduction. Being party to a developmental social fabric, it is therefore also party to global, regional and national initiatives that determine economic success (ESRF, 2006b). Global issues and initiatives such as globalization, poverty eradication, and the environment, among others have to be internalized by the sector as well (UNMP, 2005). Lands Sector Challenges that are classified as "exogenous" to the sector emanate from forces that have an epicentre outside the lands sector itself or are common to many sectors of the economy. They could also operate in a wider field outside and inside the nation. A sustainable solution to these challenges and issues can therefore be sought for the wider field first, i.e., outside the sector if it is to have a long lasting effect on the lands sector performance. Two national forces that have a profound effect on the Tanzania lands sector are: corruption; and population migration trends. A major finding of the 1996 Warioba Commission Report (WCR) was the fact that corruption in Tanzania has extended veins in all sectors of the economy, but sectors that offer rare services are more prone to corruption that others. Land delivery and control of land development are two such services of concern. The report was critical on the difficulty of acquiring land by local and foreign investors, both in rural and urban areas. It is worth recalling that at the time of the WCR, urban plots had already become a rare commodity in Tanzania for over a decade. The situation with regard to plot delivery in the period immediately after the WCR was reported in the first two Public Expenditure Review Studies of

2000/01 and 2001/02 respectively (GoT, 2001, 2002). The average number of urban plots surveyed and registered at the time stood at 8,200 for over 120 Towns and as low as 5,400 in a year. As it will be explained shortly, those that were readily available for delivery were less than half these numbers. In a nutshell, the plot delivery mechanism had collapsed compared to 12,000 and 22,000 plots in 1969 and 1972 respectively during an all-time low capacity and rudimental technology. Two factors should be pointed out here, so as to elaborate on the performance of urban land delivery at this time in the history of land administration in Tanzania. Firstly, the above tabulated record was obtained from a numerical count of approved surveys, It is noteworthy that the plots shown on approved survey plans were for the whole country and most of these did not constitute new land parcels and were not of benefit to new developers. They were a result of surveys for titling of existing developments such as government and parastatal housing and surveys for residents confronted with demolitions or resettlements from hazardous areas to special schemes such as Kinyerezi in Dar Es Salaam. Secondly, and as a glaring paradox, is the fact that at this rate of plot delivery, the City of Dar es Salaam alone was registering about 15,000 new house constructions per year. A good 95% of developers in the City therefore, obtained their land from the alternative market that was flourishing in un-acquired, unplanned, un-surveyed and un-serviced urban lands. It can be inferred here that the many informal settlements in the towns and cities of Tanzania grew at a rapid rate and the scramble for investment in serviced areas was grossly exposed to corrupt practices patronage and rent seeking. To this end, statistics in the development of spontaneous settlements in Dar Es Salaam alone indicate a steady positive growth. In a city of 2,497,940 people, growing at a rate of 4.3% and sprawling at 7% per year, the unplanned and un-serviced areas now constitute 70% of the city. In Dar Es Salaam, such settlements have increased from 16 in 1970, to 43 in 1980, to 55 in the late 1990s and to over 100 today. These are not safe and secure settlements by all standards and their rates of growth are, but alarming. A National Anti-corruption Strategy and Action Plan were developed by Government in 1999 to reverse the malady across sectors. Sector Ministries drew-up own Plans of Action to give more meaning to the national instrument by directly addressing the scourge that had been labelled as public enemy No. 1 in the national strategy. Specifically, the lands sector An Anti-corruption Action Plan (2001-2002) was prepared by the lands sector Ministry in 2000, to guide the fight against "the use of public office for private gain." The action plan acknowledged that the major grounds of corruption were: unethical behaviour in land administration, land delivery, procurement, and confusing regulations directed at an ignorant public. It consisted therefore, of four action areas, namely: (i) delivery of 20,000 new urban plots within a 14 month period in various cities and regional towns of Tanzania; (ii) review and harmonize existing laws and regulation on land use that seemed to be in conflict; (iii) raise awareness and skills whilst providing needed data and information in the delivery of services; and (iv) ensure adherence to procurement regulations and professional ethics among lands sector staff. The third public expenditure review study report (GoT, 2004) states that in an effort to satisfy the growing demands for plots, the lands sector Ministry in Government applied for a loan of 21 billion shillings in 2002/03 financial year from the Central Government to provide planned, surveyed and serviced urban plots in Boko, Bunju, Goba, Mbezi, Kwembe and Kiluvya in Kinondoni District; Pugu and Kinyerezi in Ilala; and Kigamboni and Mbagala in Temeke District. This has now become known as the 20,000 Plots Project. Land services in this project included substantial infrastructure improvements particularly roads, which have made it easy for plot beneficiaries to access their land parcels. Utility companies were encouraged to provide water, electricity, sewerage and telephones, and the municipalities were to upgrade the roads and the drainage systems to higher standards. The report states further that implementation of the 20,000 Plots Project in Dar Es salaam was expected to generated the following benefits to the Government as well as individuals: (i) an increase in Government revenue through plot auction, land rents, transfer fees, survey fees, preparation fees, deed plan fees, registration fees and premiums; (ii) Certificates of title deeds issued enable owners to mortgage their plots and secure loans from financial institutions; (iii) Reducing the un-proportionate expansion of squatter areas in Dar Es Salaam and in other towns where the project is replicated (iv) Reduce environmental negative impact emanating from squatting through land management by land parcel owners; (v) Easy expansion of social services such as schools, health centres, roads, electricity, water, telephone, religious centres and open space for gardens and play grounds; (vii) Construction of houses in delicate and hazardous areas like flood basins and steep areas will be minimized if not totally eliminated; (viii) Plot availability will facilitate construction of houses, hence shelter provision to members of the society that will lead to better health, security and higher productivity; and, of most relevance in this discussion is the fact that, (ix) Corruption related with land delivery activities would be arrested by reducing the gap between supply and demand of plots. It would be of benefit to all to make an audit of the project in terms of these envisaged benefits so as to evaluate the extent at which expectations have been met some seven years down the line.

RURAL-URBAN MIGRATION:

Migratory trends in Tanzania form a very interesting pattern. The 1978, 1988 and 2002 National censuses of Tanzania indicated that urban population was about 2.3, 4.0 and 7.9 million, respectively. The censuses indicate also that the urban population increased from 13.3% in 1978 to 17.9 % in 1988 and further to 23.1% by year 2002. It is evidenced by these figures that Tanzania is experiencing rapid urbanization in the same manner as other Sub-Saharan countries and Africa in general. The big rush was for Dar es Salaam City whose population had increases tenfold since independence in 1961. The census data for year 2002 reveals the trend that Dar es Salaam Region still continues to have positive net migration of 1,131,457 people, followed by Manyara Region (161,251), Tabora (129,965), Arusha (89,295), Rukwa (57,688) and Morogoro (49,990). Other regions that have positive net migration include Mbeya and Kagera. On the other hand, Kilimanjaro, Iringa, Tanga, Dodoma, Kigoma and Mtwara Regions are the six largest losers. By all standards, Dar Es Salaam is a primate city, endowed with the best services of any urban centre in Tanzania. As such, living in Dar Es Salaam is the dream of all who can afford to leave their ancestral homes. To many, it is the only place to earn a living. The development of urban centres in Tanzania, and Dar Es Salaam City in particular, is driven by rural-urban migration that, in turn, is fuelled by the imbalance in lifestyles between rural and urban centres and between regional towns and the Dar Es Salaam City. This dual migration syndrome has overburdened housing and all other services in the Cities and Towns of Tanzania. Jobs have dwindled fuelled by retrenchments of the same period, in the public service, shutdowns in parastatal organisations and industries as well as marginal finance for the emerging private sector of the novice market economy. Consequently, the population increase is far ahead of what the urban economies can afford, on a narrow tax base and poverty of its taxpayers. On the other side of the process are migrations away from the central plateaux and similar agro-economic zones to the eastern coastal strip (Mtatifikolo, 2004). The unfriendly drought conditions of the past post *el-nino* decade, has favoured migrations to the higher rainfall and into urban centres in the same areas. The net effect has been a population shift eastwards. Tanzania has a shortfall of natural pastureland and a surplus of arable land. Statistics show that slightly less than 55% of Tanzania land mass is comprised of arable land.

However, it is only 10.1% of the land surface is under cultivation, implying that over 81.6% of all arable land is not used for farming. The picture being painted by this statistics is that of *abundance of land as the 81.6% of arable land* is available for new occupation and use. Further, Tanzania is made up of 61,285,800 Ha of pasture out of which only 35,528,000 Ha is permanent. However, the amount of acreage used for pasture stands at about 44,003,200 Ha or some 71.8% of the non-permanent pasture or 124% of permanent pastureland. These figures also imply that a sizable proportion of grazing is undertaken on 8,475,200 Ha, of non-permanent pasture, that is vulnerable to harsh weather conditions. Pastoralists in such areas have to look elsewhere during drought times.

Population shifts involving pastoralists, moving away from ancestral areas, in search of pasture has been a source of untold land-use conflicts as has been the refugee problem in the north-western Tanzania. The 2002 census shows that the highest average population growth rate in Tanzania by Region is in Kigoma Region at 4.8% per annum as a consequence of the refugee problem. The obvious refuge for pastoralists is the wetlands in the Usangu and Kilombero valleys and generally, along the coastal strip with a higher rainfall compared to the central plateaux and several river deltas. In a historical note it is seen that the four coastal urban centres, Dar Es Salaam, Tanga, Lindi and Mtwara alone increased their share of population in Mainland Tanzania from 2.2% in 1957 to 7.4% in 1988. The picture would be more conspicuous if the other minor settlements on the coastal belt were included, as there is evidence that the growth rates of Kibaha and Bagamoyo in Pwani, Muheza and Korogwe in Tanga, are higher than average.

POLICY-DERIVED LANDS SECTOR CHALLENGES

Policy derived Challenges in the sector are defined as Challenges that are caused by weakness in policy analysis and strategic planning, inefficiency and stagnation in land administration processes. Policy derived Challenges in the lands sector include underperformance and even stagnation in: (i) land acquisition and valuation, (ii) design of land-use plans and master plans, (iii) preparation of settlement layouts, (iv) cadastral processes, (v) land delivery and registration, (vi) poor enforcement of town planning and building regulations, (vii) poor capacity building, (viii) skilled manpower retrenchments, (ix) unregulated land markets, (x) weak dispute settlement machinery and (xi) weak enforcement of law and order. This list is long because it emphasizes the pivotal role of appropriate policies in governance. The professions servicing the lands sector were not deeply rooted in Tanzania's tertiary education system at independence, although that scenario is now changing at a fast pace. Indeed, many years into independence not only were there no indigenous professional land surveyors, physical planners, valuers, or cartographers, but also there was no University that was easily accessible to Tanzanians at which courses specialized in these disciplines could be offered, in spite of provisions made in the various sub sector laws. The overwhelming capacity problem compelled Ministerial leadership to open up the sub professional programs at an Advanced Diploma level in 1974 on Observation Hill, in Dar Es Salaam and pursued a vigorous capacity building programme for the sector, including posting students in Universities abroad (GoT, 2004). It took many years to graduate students with higher degrees, through scholarships, and only in the decade of the 1980s was it possible for the country to register Doctorates in surveying related disciplines as a real milestone, and only as recent as a decade ago did the other professions follow suit.

Weak Start In Capacity Building:

Most of the senior officers in the lands sector Ministry were of British decent, shortly after independence, and almost all left the country within ten years of independence. The Lands sector operated, for a time, without professionally skilled persons, except for the few technicians trained under British rule. Consequently, the first few graduates from the University of East Africa, at Nairobi, worked and functioned without experienced supervision upon recruitment. It is on record that many new recruits occupied senior vacant position to fill an apparent vacuum rather than on merit or experience. Most lacking in the sector, as early as the late 1960s, were skills for project planning that were rarely taught in engineering faculties in the Universities of the time. The occasional use of economic planners was therefore unaided by sector professionals and became irrelevant, as it would have been expected, under the circumstances. The result of such a scenario was that a poor foundation for policy formulation, policy analysis and strategic planning in the lands sector Ministry was set very early in independent Tanzania. It must also be appreciated that poor planning often has a bearing on the relevance of activities undertaken to facilitate the attainment of goals. If goals are improperly set the performance could certainly be of marginal relevance. In the circumstances, even the goals identified are often not clearly defined due to lack of strategy. *Ad hoc* policies, strategies, and goals often lead to *ad hoc* processes that often lead to poor investment and waste of resources.

Ad Hoc Policy Reversals:

The practice in land delivery since the enactment of the Land, Town and Country Planning, Land Registration and the Land Survey Ordinances as the legal framework of the lands sector, always involved a four-step process. In urban areas land delivery logically starts with acquiring land after exhausting all third party interests and paying requisite compensation to all identified land and property owners. Secondly, physical planning processes in which layout(s), for the acquired lands, are designed in accordance with agreed land-use and settlement patterns. Thirdly, the town-planning (TP) diagrams are transferred to the ground through cadastral surveying processes that, in Tanzania, are based on fixed land parcel boundaries. The end product of cadastral surveying is the replacement, for purposes of land delivery, of the TP Drawing by a registered survey plan and corresponding data and information is archived. The registered survey plan is a legal instrument and many countries that implement land registration by registration of deeds, use the plan as the final document. Tanzania implements land registration through registration of title framed using deed plans derived from the registered survey plans. The fourth and final stage is therefore the allocation, through sale, auction or by other agreed method of all the plots in the survey plan as identified by plot numbers thereon and granting land rights to the recipients. The planning authority takes care of open spaces and recreation or special purpose grounds. Allocation is ascertained by letters of offer and, upon acceptance of the offer and payment of requisite fees, certificates of occupancy (CO) are prepared for land in the general lands. The grant of land rights process is therefore completed. In Tanzania, the order and logic of these steps were honoured for over a decade into independence. Somehow consequences of abrogating the enumerated steps were not analysed and relayed to policy makers timely and with due clarity. In the 1980s the practice broke down. Some processes were deemed unnecessary, outside professional circles, and hence were circumvented. In particular, and as rural-urban migration increased TP Drawings were prepared for un-acquired lands and political authority expected the cadastral surveys to proceed irrespective of whether or not existing rights were exhausted by paying due compensation. Discussing plot shortages in urban centres, the report on the first public expenditure reviews (GoT, 2001) stated that; "The Surveys and Mapping Division and the private sector do not attribute the (current) cause of plot scarcity to lack of human resources or equipment. … The agreed reason in the decline is essentially, unavailability of acquired, fully compensated and planned land for cadastral surveying and subsequent delivery to developers."

Land Delivery In Village Lands:

On the basis of the provisions of section 12 of the VLA, village land is divided into three classes, namely; *individual, communal and vacant* lands (GoT, 1999b). Individual land is land that is being occupied or used by an individual or family or group of persons under customary law. It includes land held under the deemed right of occupancy. Such land *is not subject to allocation by the village council* since it is already occupied (Fimbo, 2004). Communal village land is part of village land, which is occupied and used or available for occupation and use on a community and public basis. This category of land is *not available for grants of customary rights of occupancy or derivative rights.* Vacant land is land, which may be available for communal or individual occupation and use through allocation by the village council by way of customary right of occupancy or derivative rights such as leases, licences, etc. It was intended that this category of land should be available for allocation to a villager who is a citizen (by way of customary right of occupancy) or to a non-village organization as well as a non-citizen (by way of derivative right). It must be pointed out that the VLA in sections 18 and 22, reserves the customary right of occupancy to citizens and no other persons. So, the power of the village council is limited to grant of derivative rights if the applicant is a non-citizen or non-village organization (ibid.). The village council appears to have been granted exclusive jurisdiction with regard to the *vacant land* category and villagers as such have no voice on its allocation.

The village council can recommend to the Commissioner for Lands for the grant of a right of occupancy in these lands.

Village Land Registration:

Village Land registration is possible for village lands that have been adjudicated. The object of adjudication of interests in land is the determination of persons that they are entitled to customary rights of occupancy, determination of boundaries of the lands in question and recording of those persons in an adjudication record. A final adjudication record becomes part of the register of village land. In preparing the provisional adjudication record, a village adjudication committee, if it is satisfied that: a person is and has been or his predecessor in title was in peaceable, open and uninterrupted occupation of village land under customary law for not less than twelve years, shall determine that person to be entitled to a customary right of occupancy. There are numerous challenges associated with land delivery in Villages particularly where the village assembly is not involved. These include that: (i) a weak and relatively poor composition of the village council is pitied against the powerful investors in an environment of big bucks; and (ii) the method of adjudication selected has real weaknesses unless the process is taken as a start of a more rigorous method in a progressive titling scenario. It suffers from human problems such as death, emigration or a change in mind by witnesses to the process. Also, unless the adjoining land parcel owners are always in agreement, cases of shifting evidence have been reported in many areas and could cause conflicts (Lugoe, 2007). National policies and laws have left this aspect of land administration open to patronage. It is another aspect of land delivery that shows weakness in policy formulation. Many African countries particularly, of the Commonwealth of Nations, have historically defined parcel boundaries using the fixed boundary approach that recognizes and requires the application of surveyed boundaries. Adjudication should proceed to a boundary fixation process by the survey method.

Duality of Land Administration Services

The existing institutional framework is viewed, as far from being optimal for providing sustainable rural and urban land development. At the institutional level, policy derived Challenges include: (i) those associated with duality of service providers, (ii) non-decentralisation of services, (iii) disharmonious sector laws and (iv) inadequate guarantee of the sanctity of certificated titles. Land Administration in Tanzania operates under a duality system centralised at the Ministry of Lands, Housing and Human Settlements Development, and in District Land Offices that are under the Prime Minister's Office for Regional Administration and Local Government. The former provides policy and technical leadership and national implementation, the latter – district level operational implementation. There is therefore a need for an efficient institutional linkage of the two in the interest of land administration performance. Such linkage was not carefully thought out at the time of separation of duties and responsibilities. Decentralisation or devolution of services to be undertaken by the sector Ministry has been talked about with little done on the ground for some time now. The practice remains that some issues need to be referred to Dar Es Salaam where this could be done in the District if proper policies were put in place. Discussing the issue of decentralisation, SPILL states (Lugoe et al, 2005a) that operationally, the sector Ministry shall retain the regulatory framework that includes: (i) authority to examine and approve; TP drawings, cadastral surveys, and valuation reports; (ii) signing certificates of title; undertaking title verifications, adjudications, transfers and transmissions; and (iii) keeping copies of land records land-use plans and approved layout designs pertaining to the specific Districts Further, the day to day activities of the lands sector operatives within LGA at District level after decentralisation will be to: (i) establish and maintain framework and thematic data and its use in land delivery, (ii) preparation of settlement layouts, (iii) undertake valuations, (iv) administering provisions of the land and other sectoral laws, (v) village boundary surveys and (vi) dispute settlements. The nation awaits the implementation of this key strategic provision, which will make the land administration system much easier to access and reduce costs and delays to the land users.

Guaranteeing Sanctity of Titles

The new land laws have called into the open the need to review other existing laws on land matters particularly those pertaining to land administration infrastructure processes – mapping, land registration, surveying, land delivery, valuation, etc., and instituting some where there are gaps. In this undertaking the cadastral system starting at the design of settlement layouts to the issuance of titles, must be reformed and be made flexible and efficient enough as to cope with the demands placed on it by new provisions. Certificates of Occupancy (CO) offered by the CoL provide evidence that the President has alienated land rights to one of the citizens for a specific piece of land (parcel) to enjoy under conditions of tenure spelled thereon. There follows, therefore, a requirement for absolute guarantee of the sanctity of the granted rights of the registered land so that the CO can instil in the owners a feeling of security against any prejudices, interferences, encroachments, encumbrances and trespasses. They should not, at any time, think that only the courts could guarantee a derivative right. Like any other potential or real breach of individual rights, possessors of land rights ought to be saved from any possible breach of their rights by the immediate law enforcement agents, upon call. By the same token, there ought not be any difficulties, including delays and bureaucratic inefficiency, in transferring such rights upon disposition through any legal form of conveyance.

Uneven Land Services

Concentration of land development services in certain areas of the country with deficiency in others is another of the policy derived problematic issues to be addressed. For example; (i) land-use planning is concentrated in urban areas; (ii) township maps are not available in towns, except Dar es Salaam, (iii) urban maps are updated more often than rural maps and many of which are out of stock in the latter category; (iv) land registries are located at zone offices but not even at regional headquarters, making them less accessible; (v) most professional private practitioners are concentrated in the cities, with Dar Es Salaam hosting most of the physical planners, valuers, lawyers and land surveyors, followed by Arusha, Dodoma and Moshi, whilst other towns have none; (vi) the practice remains that cadastral surveys, valuation reports and TP Drawings must be approved in Dar Es Salaam and professionals must travel to the capital not only to get such work finalised but in many cases to get projects started, through data search, survey instructions, etc. There is also a need for a land policy review to firm up the implementation of the Village Land act No. 5 of 1999 that deals with village lands where the majority of Tanzanians live and where every indigenous Tanzanian calls "home". This law provides a historical reversal of a land administration system that focused on the urban and neglected, on purpose, the rural areas. Many analysts think that it is time that a Division of Village Land Development Services be established in the sector Ministry, headed by a Director, with operating offices and staff in all districts.

Dilemma with Urban Land Services:
Lands that have been allocated for the planning and development of urban centres in Tanzania are too big to be managed with ease and to be serviced with infrastructure and utilities. It is not uncommon for areas over 1000 square kilometres of urban development being set aside for the smallest of towns such as Sumbawanga. It has been learnt that in search of a municipal status for example, Tabora first sought and received an expansion of its borders to include an additional eight villages at the time. The sheer size of such urban area makes it attractive for the delivery of large

chunks of land that are sparsely distributed over the area, to developers most of whom are too poor to complete buildings to acceptable standards. It also pushes the planning authorities to allocate all the land for the sake of safety and security to the dwellers. This increases the infrastructure and utilities (roads sewage, electricity, water, garbage collection) networks and stretches common emergence services (police, ambulances, fire brigades) and other social (schools, hospitals, post offices, banks) services beyond easy access. All this is done in spite of the statement in the NLP that calls for town developments vertically. There is need to publicly debate this policy option so as to arrive at implementable actions.

Spatial Information Framework

It has been stated earlier that Tanzania's land delivery system operates on fixed boundaries, which is not possible without a rigorous system for geo-referencing boundary beacons and other land data. Such a system has a myriad of uses across sectors. A few applications are to: (i) support mapping, against which land-use and settlement planning is done, (ii) prepare information records for each and every land parcel for which a certificate of occupancy and certificate of village land are framed, etc., and (iii) facilitate engineering, and other surveys, mapping, and the creation of spatial data/information and in defence manoeuvres. Lugoe and Msemakweli (1998) have undertaken a compendium of resources available for spatial information and mapping in Tanzania. Their work reveals that the first available record on network coverage in Tanzania is given by technical circular no.4 on the Surveys and Mapping Division, authorizing the use of

477 triangulation data issued in 1956. In subsequent years, 55 more geo-referencing points were added bringing the 1965 Arc Datum Adjustment results to 532 points. The basic geo-referencing framework of Tanzania is therefore comprised of 532 points including: triangulation and lately, GPS data obtained from three separate campaigns; (i) an international effort for airports under the auspices of the Directorate of Civil Aviation (8 points); (ii) the mapping of the Mwanza Block (40 points); (iii) and the mapping of nine cities projects under the urban sector engineering project, USEP (377 points), with a cumulative total of 957 basic geo-referencing points. These account for one point for an area of about 1,000 square kilometres. The grossly inadequate provision needs a firm policy and resources to address it effectively.

Out-Dated Base Maps:

Tanzania has a long-standing national mapping programme (NMP) to avail the nation with all maps shown in the map catalogue. The mapping programme involves mapping processes that will facilitate availability of four types of products, namely: (i) the international map series at 1:1,000,000, 1:250,000 and 1:50,000; (ii) the national series at medium and large scales including township maps, regional and district maps; (iii) thematic maps such as the tourist maps, road maps, and 1:1000,000 map of Kilimanjaro; and (iv) Atlas pages for national atlases. These national mapping needs are documented in the national mapping catalogue. An expensive component of mapping stems from the need to map the relief that is vital in all water and drainage related projects, projects requiring earthworks, irrigation agriculture, road design and construction, etc. The economic developments that require only a marginal knowledge of the relief such as aspects of land use planning, physical planning and regularisation of settlements, forestry, agriculture, telecommunications etc, may be done much faster by using imagery from digital aerial photography controlled by the global positioning system (GPS) or by satellite imagery (un=rectified). Acquisition of land cover imagery now has to be seen as a part of NMP. Some of the maps particularly, those in the small and medium scale categories require a national coverage and constant availability and be updated regularly. Few maps in Tanzania meet these quality criteria. The large-scale maps are earmarked for selected areas of rapid development such as urban centres and settlements, where the 1:2,500 scale is relevant. Of particular importance is the 1:50,000 medium scale national cover that has been adopted worldwide as base map for economic planning and development. Due to its importance in availing all sectors of the economy with a model of the landscape on which to plan and design various economic and engineering activities, the national base map need always to be in print and be updated at most after 8 years i.e. 1/8 of the territory to be photographed and mapped every year.

OTHER CHALLENGES

These include: (i) the decay of existing maps; (ii) delays in the production of maps for areas already photographed resulting in the production of already decayed maps; (iii) maps being consistently out of print for lack new editions and (iv) breaking down of the antiquated map printing equipment.

The Unknown Landscape:

Challenges in base mapping are of several types, namely: (i) There are unmapped gaps whose only remedy is a mapping through all the activities of aerial photography, photographic control, machine plotting, cartographic processes and map production; (ii) Some existing map sheets are only provisional, particularly in the Coast and Morogoro Blocks, which require new mapping and compilation; and (iii) Some maps are so old that units thereon are still imperial. The national 1:50,000 base map series for Tanzania consists of 1265 map sheets compiled from aerial photographs. However, only 1255 sheets have ever been, mapped. There are 14 provisional sheets of the Tanganyika series in the northeast and, another approximately 12500 square kilometre of landscape has never been mapped, though photographed. The latter consists of the 8 map sheets of Kiomboi area in Singida Region and 2 sheets in Kagera Region. A unique phenomenon to Tanzania is the out datedness of nearly all maps published prior to the villagisation of the country in early 1970s, due to age and re-situating of resettlements. The present location of these villages, the infrastructure between them, corresponding changes in land-use patterns are therefore not mapped to date, except in the Mwanza-Geita block. This is an issue of great concern particularly, to land-use planning, rural development and must be closely examined also in context of national rural development strategy (RDS) and the agricultural sector development strategy (ASDS).

Urban Mapping Programme

The mapping of townships is the subject of the national urban mapping programme (NUMP) that aims at providing and updating maps in major settlements of the country. Some 104 townships are included in the NUMP and are mapped at scales 1:2500 in colour, when resources permit. Most recent maps in this series are monochrome and therefore leave much to be desired. Of note also is that only a few of the townships have maps compiled from aerial photographs that are less than 8 years old. The rate of map production is very slow and, at this rate of production the map revision exercise will lag far behind the decay deadline. Resources must be made available to change this scenario so as to revise the township maps in 5-year cycles. This requires constant aerial photography and subsequent operations at a rate of 21 townships per year if mapping is to be in tune with national development. A case in point is the situation is Dar Es Salaam in which most suburbs located over 10 kilometres from the central business district are not displayed on any of the 1:2500 map sheets of the City.

Spatial Data Infrastructure (NSDI) Development

More recent data sets of relevance to the SDI initiative in Tanzania have been derived from research and donor funded projects. Their standards and reference systems are as varied as the researchers and donors themselves. It is obvious that there has been duplication of efforts in collecting SD among various data providers and users in Tanzania, which in turn imply wasteful of scarce financial resources and possible inconsistencies.

In Tanzania, the usual way to find out which organizations have some needed data is by visiting the respective offices. There is so much information amongst the various spatial data producers but no structured ways to keep track of where, how and what is available exist. Thus this establishment will serve time resource that is usually lost in the course of searching the appropriate place for finding applicable data for the activity in hand. (Lugoe and Yanda, 2007). The need for the establishment of national SDI is also crucial currently due to its potential benefits to the local communities. There are main public interests and activities that are performed nationally but are implemented locally and thus affect the communities in various ways. These include community protection; census; health planning in terms of services catchment areas; community services including education, employment, recreation and tourism; transportation including routs; Agriculture including crop and feed management, yield planning and forecasting, weather and rainfall, and soil / land management; and in mineral resources covering mineral extraction, exploration, mining leases and geology. The establishment of National SDI will also encourage the increasing of community participation in the discussions of these pertinent issues due to readily availability of appropriate data (ibid.). Coping with all the above-mentioned SDI constraints and, more importantly, the increased demand for cross policies it is time for Tanzania to reconsider and endorse the effective establishment and management of the national SDI. Additionally, the use of SDI in decision making and in the implementation of national and sector polices in the country should be emphasized as the nation strives to attain sustainable development and reducing poverty levels amongst her people. Sustainable development and economic decision making requires spatial or geo-referenced information.

FINANCE

The lands sector experienced serious financial difficulties in the past forty years in spite of more demands that were placed on its services during the same time. It is unimaginable how a country could embark upon a grandiose project such as villagisation without the right maps and the right land-use plans for the whole country. By financial constraint it is to be understood gross under-funding of sector initiatives and activities, even when the objectives at which the activities are directed are well known and the use of resourced are well understood. Under-funding and under-investment severely hamper performance and efficiency particularly, as it pertains to the custody of land records, procurement of topographical mapping, land-use planning and cadastral surveying services as well as the acquisition of working tools for GIS, LIS and equipment for surveys, mapping, physical planning, record keeping and information dissemination. In Tanzania, these imported tools of labour are obtained with difficulty. The lands sector has had a record collection in revenue over a number of years now, but there has not been a corresponding level of ploughing back into the system to substantially ease this situation in the public sector particularly in District offices. Land use planning, for example, is hampered by the absence of current land cover and topographical maps and the same is true in planning settlement layouts. Where the latter has been accomplished on old aerial photography or maps, the exercise of transferring the designs to the ground has been cumbersome, expensive, inefficient and time consuming as most layouts do not adequately tally with ground truth. Paradoxically, the 20,000 Plots project that operates on a revolving fund at cost recovery policy is proving to be a great success. Why can't other products be delivered under the same or modified form or similar policy?

Suspension of Key Sector Activities:
The historical development of the sector reveals that many of the basic and expensive needs of the sector were neglected as a consequence of budgetary squeeze and absence of development partners. Corresponding interventions that were suspended very early in

independent Tanzania include: (i) development of National, Regional and District framework Land-use Plans; (ii) small scale map revision and medium scale mapping; (iii) revision and development of the national geo-referencing framework; (iv) delivery of planned, surveyed and serviced plots commensurate with the demand; (v) due redress of the proliferation of irregular settlements; and unplanned urban sprawls. Challenges in sector financing are responsible for the continuing omissions of many activities and interventions from the Ministerial Budgets. Non-traditional activities that are deemed important in addressing national poverty reduction measures cannot be easily included. It is not possible now to find many sector needs listed in the MTEF costing matrices due to low budget ceilings that are set each year on the basis of previous budgets and the overall national budget envelope, even as recent and periodic national proclamations continue to point to the lands sector as a "core sector" in national development efforts and poverty reduction strategies. A comprehensive costing of lands sector needs performed recently show that an average of 30 billion shillings are required annually for the next ten years if the sector is to provide normal services to the economy and address poverty reduction as expected. Many needs constitute one-time and lifetime expenses. The frameworks for geo-referencing, mapping, land-use planning, once completed, need regular maintenance that is relatively cheaper, whilst some services such as the land delivery chain (physical planning, property adjudication, cadastral surveying, valuation, development control and titling) are capable of cost recovery with a possibility of making profit for revenue generation.

Missed Opportunities

It has been shown that land-based challenges are many in number and include: (i) an old mind-set on a modern land dispensation as discussed earlier. The general lack of awareness among many actors, particularly at the village and district levels, regarding the history of reforms in the country and achievements accomplished in land regulation; (ii) Lack of will to address obvious trespass and encroachment as provided for in the laws. These challenges result in inaction. The roaming of the countryside by some pastoralists with little regard to existing land rights is a case to consider. Also inaction to protect loss of crops and livestock against theft is fuelled by this lack of will to act; (iii) Poor enforcement of rules and regulations manifests itself in the preferred mode of top-down planning rather than the participatory. Also the, low capacity for development control that has left open spaces and way leaves prone to invasion is considered, as is an increase in land-use conflicts and disputes both in rural and urban areas; and (iv) A face value guarantee for land titles that manifests itself in law enforcement agents, particularly the police, not intervening directly in incidences of criminal trespass. Land administrators encourage court action rather than executive action that could offer quick solutions particularly, when land titles are openly questioned. (v) Massive growth of irregular settlements. There are housing constructions springing up in unplanned, un-surveyed and un-serviced areas of most urban areas including settlement in hazardous lands as well as open spaces and way leaves or for recreation and public land-use; (vi) land administration authority is far detached from land users and a call is therefore to decentralize down to the Districts so as to also give easy and prompt access to records, maintained at headquarters in Dar Es Salaam, and to the various authorizations stated in law; (vii) Land administration system is part of Government that operates a dual system of services, i.e. in the lands sector Ministry and in local government. The latter often undertakes land delivery activities in a relatively weak institutional framework; (viii) The New Land Laws and supporting sub sector laws are not always in sync with other sector laws on minerals, water, agriculture, infrastructure developments, etc., and need to be harmonized, bearing in mind the primacy of the former; (ix) The market in land is not regulated and still operates as an informal activity. The wide spread sale of land without a framework to guide such sales and protecting the vulnerable, including regulation of real estate agents and making provision for leasing agricultural lands; (vi) continuing patronage and corruption in the procurement and delivery of services.

The Challenges cited in preceding discussions have infringed upon land distribution and access opportunities, which are major interventions of the sector. The Challenges have also denied due security of tenure and conversely, unleashed disputes and conflicts upon holders of land rights and users which have obstructed opportunities for economic growth and reduction of poverty both at micro and macro levels. Settlements in the country are not planned for optimal land use that could be expensive to remedy in the future.

Wealth Embedded In Properly Administered Land

A missed opportunity has been on ignorance to realize the fact that land is not only a source of wealth for all who invest in it but is itself wealth if properly exploited. Secure land rights provide a sense of belonging to the land that in turn enables the owners to conserve and manage the land productively. An excerpt in the National Geographic Society (NGS) magazine no.4 of 1998 is worth quoting here: *"fifty years ago … an acre planted in onions would produce about 200 sacks per acre … of yellow onions. When we got that up to 350 sacks per acre, we thought we were the hottest thing in farming. Today if we can't produce 800 sacks per acre, we can't compete with the guy down the road"* - a foursome yield increase. Imagine what a 400% increase in incomes of rural people would do to the living conditions of rural poor at the poverty line, their families, and the country side from land that is well cared for! Can land rights be so secured as to encourage this kind of investment in Tanzania by Tanzanians?

TENURE SECURITY ENHANCES PEACE AND STABILITY

There are also opportunities for a long lasting peace that would be created by instilling proper education in the people on respecting registered lands and properties thereon. This is a lesson for every law-abiding citizen to learn. The issue of land boundaries and land rights, defined within them, should have been part and parcel of civic education in schools and to all law enforcement agencies. Much destruction to property, through overgrazing, would be avoided, as would be ensuing commotions among peoples. A case in point is the dispute among villages of Usa River vs. Imbaseli; Imbaseli vs. Nkwaranga, Imbaseli vs. Ngwalekoli regarding an Estate in Poli Division along Usa-Momela Road and its apportioning to the various villages reported to the author in 2004. A primary school located on the farm had to be abandoned by the nearby village out of threats made by disputing parties.

AGRICULTURE - ADVANTAGES TO SURROUNDING POPULATIONS:

Investment in large-scale farming creates jobs to those who cannot afford capital for farming on their own; through wage employment as have been for many years on sisal, coffee and tea plantations. There is also the ripple effect to smallholder agriculturalists that make use of opportunities created by large farms as evidenced on cane sugar, tea and coffee farming on lands surrounding processing plants. Though not directly employed by the plantations, the smallholder agriculturalists make use of a ready market created for them by large farms. There is also evidence of increased opportunities for microfinance accessed by these agriculturalists that would have not been made available had the private plantations not invested among them. Financing and lending institutions increase their businesses, which progressively increase with availability of collateral when the farms are issued with certificates of title.

SECTOR PRODUCTS ENABLE DECISION SUPPORT SYSTEMS

Missed opportunities exist across sectors as linkages and synergies weaken with diminished services from the lands sector.

Lands Sector products include geo-referencing information in the form of spatial data and maps. These products constitute data and information that is an indispensable decision support system. It is integrated with socio-economic data to enhance decision-making in development planning. It is particularly handy to the design and implementation of various engineering projects, defence preparedness, tourism, etc. One area that is almost void of such data in Tanzania is Kiomboi District through which passes the Singida-Shelui section of the Singida-Nzega Road that is now under construction. Preparations for construction work, financed by the World Bank, started in 1992 but the design could not be agreed upon until 2004 – a 12-year period. Investigations carried out in 2002 unveiled gross error in the data that was used by the designer as obtained from the data custodians at the Surveys and Mapping Division. Further, there was no ground reference to check on the errors at the time because the area has no base maps. All data had to be generated on site at a great cost to the project.

UNDER-FUNDING AFFECTS OTHER SECTORS

When the programme for the survey of villages was initiated in the Southern Regions and elsewhere, it relied on existing out-dated aerial photographs, as technology was not availed to the project because of financial constraints. The work done to survey 2,828 villages was declared to be below standard and hence was to be repeated. Financing was assured only when villages in eleven out of the then 20 Regions in the project was placed under the Forest Resources Management Project (FRMP). The village survey programme was tremendously accelerated by the acquisition of the Global Positioning System (GPS) technology, and as such it is envisaged that by end of 2007 all 10,500 villages in the country will have been surveyed. Recalling that village surveys are a prerequisite to issuance of Certificates of Village Lands, which are a condition precedent to individualised titling within the village, financing for appropriate technology translates into certificates of village lands and into opportunities to enjoy customary land rights in these lands. It has been reported that villagers availed with certificates of customary rights of occupancy are now accessing credit in financing institutions and are able to meaningfully invest in land development.

Planned Sites and Situations Of Villages:

The location of villages during the villagization programme could have benefited abundantly if a national land-use mapping, aimed at identifying optimal areas that are endowed with characteristics conducive to village livelihoods, was undertaken as a condition precedent. This opportunity was lost and, for some villages, it might be lost forever due to high costs of relocations. In the planning of rural settlements, it is important to pay attention to the sites and situations of the villages, aided by appropriate tools particularly the base maps that should be supplemented by geological, soil and land cover maps. Good sites of settlements involve an assessment of the land in terms of its soils, vegetation, topography, relief, geographical location and orientation. It is not uncommon to find Tanzania villages, particularly in the Kilombero valley, occupying the best agricultural soils and sometimes, surrounded by less fertile ones. A settlement situation is its position with respect to surrounding areas and other settlements from which it could benefit economically through infrastructural links. Again, it is not uncommon to find villages that cannot be accessed easily and often, in lack of vital supplies and services especially, during rains. Although this situation can be remedied, it is often at a great expense, like providing basic services (water, schools, dispensaries, roads, police posts, post offices, etc) where these could have been shared with neighbouring villages. An alternative to providing services is to relocate. But, often many a village are less facilitated and hence disadvantaged as a result.

Avoiding Land-Use Conflicts:

Of greater worry are opportunities missed in linking the sites and situations to means of livelihoods. Semi-dry areas are better suited to pastoralism than agriculture - occupations, which have been practiced as part of traditions and would not part with them in spite of unfriendly geographical and environmental condition. In essence, this has also been a missed opportunity that has led to conflicts between agriculturalists and pastoralists, in the past two decades. As agriculturalists increase their activities for want of more income and as a result of their population growth, pastoralists move outward to better pasture and as a result their herds increase wanting more land that is not available after being infringed upon by farmers. Pastoralists then start moving

and in the process tramp upon crops and
occupy non-ancestral lands irrespective
of existing land rights.

Chapter 6: BEGINNING OF REAL LAND REFORMS:

In the late 1980s and early 1990s, it was felt that there was a need to develop a coherent and comprehensive land policy that would define the land tenure structure and enable proper land management and allocation in light of profound economic and social changes that had been taking place since Independence. In particular, a new land policy was needed to:

- Accommodate changes in land use and increase in human population;
- Control large livestock population which increases demand for grazing land and creates serious land degradation;
- Protect the environment from extension of cultivation to marginal areas;

- Reduce conflicts in land-use between agriculturalists and pastoralists and between various land-users and the environment particularly, forest and wildlife areas and water sources;

- Provide for increased urbanization requiring lands for settlements, industries and commerce and preserve valuable agriculture land;

- Facilitate prospective investors who require land as a result of liberalization of the economy and investment promotion;

- Regularize the effects of the 1971-1976 villagization program (Operation Vijiji) on customary land tenure;

- Protect individual land rights under a pluralistic political system since 1992; and

- Accommodate various court decisions affirming customary land rights of the local people.

Moreover, the evaluation of customary tenure towards more individualized ownership accompanied by the development of land markets in areas where land is scarce and cash crops such as coffee, tea and wheat are grown mainly on individual holdings (e.g., Ukerewe, Rungwe, Lushoto, Moshi, Arumeru and Bukoba Districts) called for a more pragmatic land policy to accommodate the needs of the people and the economy.

PRESIDENTIAL COMMISSION OF INQUIRY INTO LAND MATTERS

The President appointed the Commission of Inquiry into Land Matters in 1991, under the chair of Professor Issa Shivji of the University of Dar Es Salaam. The main task was to assess the existing policies and conditions concerning the allocation, use, tenure and development of land and recommend a new land tenure structure, including its institutional and legal framework. However, not all recommendations presented by the Commission in 1992 were adopted. In particular, the recommendation regarding the diversification of the source of radical title (i.e., from the President to an independent National Land Commission for national lands and the village assemblies for village lands), were not instituted as a national policy. The recommendations of the National Workshop on Land Policy held at Arusha in January 1995 and comments and suggestions received from the Government, Non-Governmental Organisations and the public, culminated into the National Land Policy (NLP) of 1995.

THE NATIONAL LAND POLICY:

The overall objectives of the 1995 land policy are to: (i) promote and ensure a secure land tenure system; and (ii) encourage the optimal use of land to facilitate broad-based social and economic development without endangering the ecological balance of the environment. Its specific objectives were realised in the 15 fundamental Principles of the National Land Policy. The new land policy has the following four salient features: (i) They provide for a market in land; (ii) They create national customary land tenure and give customary rights in land the deserving weight; (iii) Embodying a traditional idea that land is a resource both owned by and due to all, they secure existing (customary) rights in land and facilitate equitable access and distribution and (iv) They vest most control over land tenure administration at the grassroots in the hands of the village councils elected by the members of each registered village.

NEW LAND ACTS OF PARLIAMENT

The fundamental principles of the National Land Policy were incorporated into the Land Act and the Village Land Act both passed by Parliament in February 1999. The former Act deals with "general land" including urban areas and private estates outside the customary sector while the latter deals with "village land". The Village Land Acts can be considered more innovative. This is not only because the vast majority of land and land holding in Tanzania falls within the class of village land but also because the most significant changes as to how rights in land may be owned and how tenure will be administered are set out by this law.

However, the two laws should be seen together as part of a whole since they were initially combined but later divided for greater digestibility. The Land Acts have provided a new regime for controlling and managing land tenure administration, repealing ten previous laws including the 1923 Land Ordinance (CAP 113). The new laws came into operation in May 2001.

Strategic Plan For The Implementation Of The Land Laws

The Strategy was designed using a validated consultative process to enable ownership and internalisation by both the Government and the population at large. A scientifically selected sample took into consideration the great diversity in cultures, incomes, geographical spread, and aspirations of Tanzanians, with regard to land tenure. Tanzania Mainland, with a total population of 33.6

million in 2002, is divided into 21 Regions, 117 Districts, about 2570 Wards and 12,000 villages out of which 10,500 are registered villages. The sample consisting of 13 Regions, 60 villages in 15 Wards and Districts were selected and used in the study. This sample was supplemented by another sample consisting of MDAs, LGA, NGOs, CBOs and CSOs located in Dar Es Salaam. The idea in identifying and ultimately selecting sampling zones was to capture the much administrative, economic, social, cultural and occupational diversity, which have direct bearing on the ultimate implementation of the new Land Laws and possibly other related Legislation. In this sample were included: (i) Rich/Average/Poor regions; (ii) Large scale commercial and smallholder (subsistence and commercial) agriculture regions; (iii) predominantly agricultural and largely livestock regions; (iv) Remote and well exposed regions; (v) Large and small urban centres and Villages in transition to 'small town' status in the chosen regions. In addition, all the agro-ecological zones were represented.

REFERENCES

1. AUC-ECA-AfDB Consortium (2010). "Framework and Guidelines on Land Policy in Africa – A framework to Strengthen Land Rights, Enhance Productivity and Secure Livelihoods". Addis Ababa, Ethiopia

2. Boudreaux, K. and D. Sacks (2009). "Mercatus on Policy: Land Tenure Security and Agricultural Productivity" Publication No. 57, Mercatus Centre, George Mason University.

3. Centre for Land, Economy and Rights of Women (CLEAR, 2005). "Land Policies in sub-Saharan Africa". Nairobi

4. Dale, P. F. (1976). "Cadastral Surveys within the Commonwealth." Her Majesty's Stationery Office. Overseas Research Publication No. 23. London.

5. Dale, P. F. and McLaughlin, J. (1999). "Land Administration". Oxford University Press. Oxford.

6. De Soto, Hernando. 2000. The Mystery of Capitalism: Why Capitalism Triumphs in the West and Fails Everywhere Else. London: Bantam Press.

7. Economic Commission for Africa (1998). "An Integrated Geo-Information (GIS) with Emphasis On Cadastre and Land Information Systems (LIS) for Decision Makers in Africa – Working Document". Addis Ababa.

8. EU (2004). "EU Land Policy Guidelines – Guidelines for Support to Land Policy Design and Land Policy Reform Processes in Developing Countries". Task Force on Land Tenure (2004). Brussels.

9. FAO (2012). "Voluntary Guidelines on the Responsible Governance of Tenure of Land, Fisheries and Forests in the Context of National Food Security." FIG Congress.

10. Fimbo, G. M. (2004). "Land Law Reforms in Tanzania." Lecture Delivered

in Commemoration of 60th Birthday." University of Dar Es Salaam.

11. Hassan, A. (undated). "The Types of Land Ownership and the Application of Land Laws in Zanzibar". Zanzibar Law Society. Zanzibar

12. Larsson, G. (1991). "Land Registration and Cadastral Systems – Tools for Land Information Management". Longman Scientific and Technical, England. John Wiley & Sons, New York.

13. LHRC & ZLSC (2011). Tanzania Human Rights Report 2010. Legal and Human Rights Centre and Zanzibar Legal Services Centre. Dar Es Salaam, Tanzania

14. Lugoe, F. (2011). "Aligning and Harmonizing the Livestock and Land Policies of Tanzania". ESRF Working Paper, Dar Es Salaam

15. Lugoe, F. (2012). "Sector Study on Land Markets in Zanzibar". RGZ/SMOLE Land Policy Development Initiative. Zanzibar

16. Lugoe, F. (2012). "Sector study on Land Disputes in Zanzibar". RGZ/SMOLE Land Policy Development Initiative. Zanzibar

17. Manji, A. (1998). "Gender and the Politics of the Land policy reform Process in Tanzania." The Journal of Modern African Studies. U.K.

18. Revolutionary Government of Zanzibar (RGZ,). "The Tourism Act of Zanzibar."

19. Revolutionary Government of Zanzibar (RGZ, 1984). "The Constitution of Zanzibar". Zanzibar

20. Revolutionary Government of Zanzibar (RGZ, 1989). "The registered Land Act." Zanzibar

21. Revolutionary Government of Zanzibar (RGZ, 1992). "The Land Tenure Act – legal supplement (part I) to the Zanzibar Government Gazette Vol. CII No. 3635 of 20th November 1993". Zanzibar

22. Revolutionary Government of Zanzibar (RGZ, 1994). "The Land Transfer Act." Act No. 8 of 1994. Zanzibar

23. Revolutionary Government of Zanzibar (RGZ, 2000). "The Zanzibar Vision 2020". Zanzibar

24. Revolutionary Government of Zanzibar (RGZ, 2009). "Draft Land Policy Zanzibar". MWCEL, Zanzibar

25. Revolutionary Government of Zanzibar (RGZ, 2010). "The Zanzibar Strategy for Growth and Reduction of Poverty (ZSGRP): 2010 – 2015, MKUZA II". Zanzibar

26. RGZ (1984). "The Constitution of Zanzibar". Zanzibar

27. RGZ (1989). "The registered Land Act." Zanzibar

28. RGZ (1992). "The Land Tenure Act – legal supplement (part I) to the Zanzibar Government Gazette Vol. CII No. 3635 of 20th November 1993". Zanzibar

29. RGZ (1994). "The Land Transfer Act." Act No. 8 of 1994. Zanzibar

30. RGZ (2000). "The Zanzibar Vision 2020". Zanzibar

31. RGZ (2009). "Draft Land Policy Zanzibar". MWCEL, Zanzibar

32. RGZ (2010). "The Zanzibar Strategy for Growth and Reduction of Poverty (ZSGRP): 2010 – 2015, MKUZA II". Zanzibar

33. SMOLE (2004). "Report of Legal Advisor's Second Mission". Zanzibar

34. Tanzania-Sweden Local Management of Natural Resources Programme (TS, 2000). "Land Administration and Mapping to Support the Implementation of the

Land Policy and the Land Acts in Tanzania". Publication no. 18 with appendices. March 2000.

35. The UN Millennium Project (UNMP, 2005). "Preparing National Strategies to Achieve the MDGs: A Handbook". At info@unmillenniumproject.org

36. Torhonen, M. (1998). "A Thousand and One Nights of Land Tenure – The Past, Present and Future of Land Tenure in Zanzibar". RICS, London.

37. UN-HABITAT (2008). "Secure Land Rights". Nairobi

38. URT (2010). "National Sample Census of Agriculture, 2007/2008" Preliminary Report. NBS, Ministry of Finance, Dar Es Salaam.

39. URT (2011). "Tanzania in Figures 2010" NBS, Ministry of Finance, Dar Es Salaam

40. Van den Brink, Rogier, Glen Thomas, Hans Binswanger, John Bruce and Frank

Byamugisha (2006) "Consensus, Confusion, and Controversy – Selected Land Reform Issues in Sub-Saharan Africa" World Bank Working Paper No. 71. Washington

41. World Bank (2003). "Land Policies for Growth and Poverty Reduction - A World Bank Policy Research Report." Oxford University Press.

ABOUT THE AUTHOR

 Dr. Furaha Lugoe is a Tanzanian national and Geodesist cum Geomatician by profession. He is author of over 120 publications. In academia, Dr. Furaha Lugoe gained a 15 year-experience in teaching and research in the fields of geomatics and geodesy at the Universities of Dar-Es-salaam (UDSM), New Brunswick (UNB), Zimbabwe (UZ) and the now Ardhi University, with links to universities in UK and Germany. In private practice has worked as land surveyor and advisor for many years. For about 30 years now, Dr. Lugoe has been active in land administration, natural resources and human settlements policy and strategy matters. Dr Furaha Lugoe has a wide

consulting and publication record and experience. Share his works on line:

www.dilaps.or.tz/downloads.php ; http://www.dilaps.or.tz/listfolderitems.php?type=10; http://www.topocarto.co.tz/downloads.php ; http://www.topocarto.co.tz/listfolderitems.php?type=miscellaneous